SANDHURST TO THE KHYBER
1932 – 1940

The author in full dress after a levee at St James' Palace, 1937.

Sandhurst To The Khyber
1932–1940

Pre-war Service With Gurkhas

by

Lieutenant Colonel Tony Mains
2nd Battalion 9th Gurkha Rifles

The Memoir Club

© A.A. Mains 1999

First published in 1999 by
The Memoir Club
The Old School
New Road
Crook Town
Durham

British Library Cataloguing in
Publication Data.
A catalogue record for this book
is available from the
British Library.

ISBN: 1 84104 007 X

Typeset by George Wishart & Associates, Whitley Bay.
Printed by Bookcraft (Bath) Ltd.

To the Memory of

The British Officers, Gurkha Officers and Riflemen
of The Gurkha Brigade of the British Indian Army

Acknowledgements

My grateful thanks first of all to my wife, Pauline, for once again reading the typescript and making corrections and suggestions; next, to General Sir Sam Cowan, Colonel Commandant of the Brigade of Gurkhas for writing the Foreword which greatly encouraged me. Finally to Patric Emerson of the Bombay Grenadiers for checking the chapters on Sandhurst and service on the Unattached List Indian Army and to Roland Buchanan of my Regiment for doing the same for the two Frontier chapters.

Contents

List of Illustrations

Foreword

by

General Sir Sam Cowan, KCB, CBE

Colonel Commandant the Brigade of Gurkhas

STORIES ABOUT LIFE in British India and service in its Army have an enduring appeal. They are worlds which many recognise and aspire to know better and in these memoirs, written with a light but sure touch, Tony Mains gives us the opportunity to do just that. He does so by drawing on his personal experience of pre-war India, and his eye for illuminating detail of scene, character and situation, with a well attuned sense of humour and the ridiculous, add greatly to the sheer pleasure of reading what he has written.

His opening account of his school days at Malvern College and of being a Gentleman Cadet at the Royal Military College Sandhurst set the scene in recalling social and military worlds which seem even further from today than the sixty-five years represented. The extended chapters on his pre-war service in India are the heart of the book. By acute and often amusing description and comment, they bring to life many aspects of what it was like to live and serve in the great military cantonments and famous hill stations of northern India. Powerful resonant names such as Dehra Dun, Poona and Simla feature prominently. People and their behaviour, attractive and unattractive, are given appropriate attention.

However, this is not simply a general account of life in the old Indian Army. Like all who served in it, Tony Mains believes that he belonged to a special part of it, and to the best part of that! In his case, the Gurkha Brigade and his own Regiment, the 9th Gurkha Rifles. As the title indicates, the book is above all a record of service with Gurkhas and all who read it will understand more about the character of Gurkhas and the special nature of service in a Gurkha regiment. Eyebrows may be raised about some of his remarks which make comparisons between soldiers who serve in the 9th Gurkhas and the clans and tribes serving in other Gurkha regiments but these simply reflect regimental pride and rivalry as well as the rich cultural and ethnic diversity of the hill people of Nepal. All who have had the privilege of serving with Gurkhas will confirm what he says about the singular demands and great sense of satisfaction of soldiering in a Gurkha regiment, not least the exceptionally strong bonds of loyalty and affection which hold together all who serve in one.

His concluding chapter on his old Regiment's service in today's Indian Army reveals the excellent links which exist between British and Indian officers despite the divide of Independence. It also correctly highlights the distinctive and distinguished place which Gurkhas continue to occupy in the Indian Army, as indeed they do, though in smaller numbers, in the British Army.

So the Gurkha story continues but these highly readable memoirs cast a warm glow on a brief but important period of a glorious past. They are so clearly written by a man devoted to his Regiment, who knows and loves its soldiers, and it is a pleasure to commend it to you.

Preface

My Family Background

M<small>Y FAMILY WAS OF</small> Scottish origin, being of Clan Menzies – my great grandfather was from County Argyll and one of seven children, who, with the exception of himself, never married or left Scotland; by dint of hard work and possessing considerable ability, he became an Attorney of Queen's Bench and Common Pleas specialising in railway matters mainly for the Great Western. My grandfather was educated at King's College School in London and followed his father into the Law, retiring finally in 1919 as Deputy Solicitor of the London and North Western Railway. He lived in a large Victorian house at Grove Park Chiswick between the London and South Western Railway's station and the River Thames. He was comfortably off, employing three servants together with a part time gardener and charlady.

My father was educated as a day boy at St Paul's School and Brasenose College, Oxford, where he achieved a Boxing 'Blue'. He also entered the Law, becoming a Barrister of the Inner Temple, and held a Commission in the 3rd County of London Yeomanry (Sharpshooters). At St Paul's, he was a contemporary of Field Marshal Montgomery, whose parents lived nearby, and the two boys on their way to school were often given a lift to Chiswick Park Station by my maternal grandfather who lived next door to the Montgomerys. My father married the daughter of Francis Barker, the youngest brother of Sir John Barker Bt., the founder of Barkers of Kensington; he joined the Parliamentary Bar and was a pupil of Sir John Simon. By December 1913, when I was born, everything seemed set fair for him.

However tragedy struck – he was mobilised in 1914, and transferred to the Royal Artillery but was invalided out after the Somme. Instead of returning to the Bar, where those barristers who had not joined up were coining money, he quixotically took a job of national importance in the Ministry of National Service. At the same time my mother became seriously ill with tuberculosis, and later, 'Spanish' flu, from which she nearly died. The doctors advised that she should be removed permanently to a warmer and drier climate. The upshot was that my father in 1919 bought a partnership in a Law firm in Salisbury, Southern Rhodesia. The difficulty then was – how could we get there? Scheduled shipping lines were only just beginning to recover after the War, so we had to go overland to Lisbon and take a Portuguese boat to Portuguese East Africa, as it was then called. My mother went ahead as far as Bordeaux and my father and I followed – my first international journey. I can remember quite a lot of it although mainly to do with food – my disappointment at being refused a second breakfast in the Pullman car *en route* to Dover and later lunch on the boat. I had my reward, dinner of fried fish and *pommes frites* at the restaurant at the Gare du Nord. Thereafter our meals in the various trains in Spain and Portugal were gorgeous picnics. I blotted my copybook in Paris at the Gare de Quai d'Orsay. My father, having installed me in our compartment of the Bordeaux *rapide*, got out to speak to Cook's representative; meanwhile a French gentleman arrived and placed his suitcase in the compartment and then also got out. This was too much for me and although only five I put his suitcase into the corridor. Luckily my father was able to pacify the Frenchman who later said that I was a '*un brave garçon*'.

The sailing of our boat was postponed so we spent some time at Estoril. The final disaster struck just after my sixth birthday, when, as we were entering Port Said, my mother died. We disembarked, and returned to England on a British India Company's steamer, the *Malda*; on our return we moved into my grandfather's house in Chiswick. This, except for a short period during my father's disastrous second marriage, became my home in England until it was blitzed in late 1940. My mother was buried at Port Said; but it is believed that the gravestone has vanished as the cemetery was fought over during the Suez adventure. I think that my father never really recovered from the shock of my mother's death and a further setback was that having been absent from the Bar for six years, he had been forgotten and his new practice was mainly confined to appearances at Magistrates' Courts; this may well have had a bearing on his death in 1936 at the early age of forty seven.

CHAPTER I

First Steps Towards an Army Career

Malvern College – Sandhurst Entrance Examination

I WAS EDUCATED AT Neville Holt preparatory school near Uppingham and at Malvern College. I was not particularly good at games and I came to a soccer public school from a rugger prep school. There was a rugger house competition in the Easter Term but regrettably no colours were awarded, although I was in the House side for four of my five years. My main interest was in the 'Corps', the Malvern College Officers' Training Corps.

The Malvern Corps had been raised at the boys' request in 1883 as an artillery unit armed with 9 pdr muzzle loading guns pulled by horses hired from the local coal merchant; from 1894 to 1914 it was unique as the only school artillery unit although, for the last five or so years of its existence as such, the guns were deemed unsafe to fire. After conversion to Infantry it was affiliated to the Worcestershire Regiment and wore their badge. The Officers were masters with Territorial Commissions but the real strength of the Corps were the three retired Warrant Officers. Two were part time, one an old gentleman with pendulous cheeks from the Worcesters, somewhat of a figure of fun and always known by his nickname of 'Chow', the second, Harper, from the Essex Regiment was the School PT and boxing instructor, and the full time member, who ran the Corps almost single handed, was Sergeant Major Wilson from the Marines. Our strength was three active and one recruit company. Joining the Corps was supposed to be voluntary, but no one ever asked me whether I wished to join, nor was any other boy asked as far as I know.

We paraded weekly – one afternoon in the winter and one evening in the summer; this was looked upon by most boys as a troublesome chore. About once a term there was a field day; I am afraid some boys

1

used to load their rifles with a steel college pen in front of a blank round and fired it at any mounted umpire who came within range – I never heard if any bulls were scored. At the end of the summer term all School Corps went to training camps staffed by the regular Army. Only boys over sixteen attended. By this reckoning, I should have attended three camps but in fact, I only attended one, the first possible; the financial stringency of the early thirties cancelled the second, and the one which would have been my last was abandoned as one of the attending schools had a case of meningitis. I learnt to smoke a pipe at my only camp – all cadets smoked if only to disguise the disgusting smell of the Army latrines. My father was keen that I should follow his example and smoke a pipe and not cigarettes; so that I should not have to break in a new pipe with the inevitable sickness, he cleaned out one of his and duly presented it to me. I can honestly say that during my smoking life I never smoked cigarettes.

I passed the Certificate 'A' examination when I was just sixteen, a year earlier than was usual, and was promoted Corporal – I had received my Lance stripe six months before on passing the practical part of the examination. Had I become a School Prefect (I was a House Prefect only), I should have become an Under Officer, but as it was I became an acting CSM before getting the almost independent post as the Sergeant in charge of the recruit platoon.

My scholastic career was very much of a switchback, but I managed to obtain the School Certificate with five credits – English, History, Geography, French and Elementary Maths.

Now was the time to make up my mind about a career, as the Vth and VIth Forms specialized. In ascending order of preference they were – University to read History, University to read Law, but equal top, the Traffic Branch of a Railway, or the Army. I had been a railway enthusiast from my prep school days and it would have been easy, with my grandfather's connections, for me to become a premium traffic apprentice on the Southern Railway. However laziness now played a part; I would have had to leave school then and there to become a railway apprentice, but I would not have to take the Army examination for another two years – the Army won, but at that time I had no ideas about the Indian Army.

There were four ways of becoming an Army Officer in 1932 –

from University, from a Territorial Army Commission, from the ranks, or, for the majority, a cadetship at either the Royal Military Academy at Woolwich, for Artillery, Engineers or Signals, or from the Royal Military College at Sandhurst for Cavalry, Infantry or Tanks. The entrance examination was conducted by the Civil Service Commissioners and was the same not only for the Army but also for entry into the Royal Marines, and the Indian and Colonial Police Forces. The difference was only in regard to age limits for entry and subjects to be taken.

The year at Woolwich and Sandhurst was split into two terms commencing in February and September; the course consisted of three terms, junior, intermediate and senior. An applicant had to be eighteen at the time of entry, so he could sit the examination twice only. The examination was competitive in that only so many cadetships were on offer, but the number and type of optional subjects varied. For the hundred and fifty vacancies at Sandhurst any two optional subjects could be selected, but for the fifty vacancies at Woolwich, three had to be taken of which two had to be Lower Mathematics and Physics plus Chemistry, and a 40 per cent mark was required in each. It was possible to take the one examination for both establishments. I did this as my father was very keen that I should join the Royal Artillery; my optional subjects, therefore, were History, Lower Mathematics and Physics plus Chemistry. I was good at the first but not at the latter two, particularly Lower Maths, which being Statics and Dynamics was largely beyond my comprehension.

I took the examination in November 1931, and duly failed Lower Mathematics, but I got a very high place for Sandhurst, twelfth, which also gave me a Prize Cadetship of £25 per annum while I was at the College. The more sensible course would have been to accept that place, rather than to try again for Woolwich with the resultant six months loss of seniority, but my father suggested that I remained at Malvern with Maths tuition in the holidays. I did not argue against this as the life of a Prefect at a Public School at that time was such that one did not want to give it up in a hurry. I regret that I did little to improve my Maths with the inevitable result – a fail for Woolwich but fifth and a Prize Cadetship for Sandhurst. My father might have been very annoyed had it not been for my Form Master, who wrote to him saying bluntly that even if I had squeezed into Woolwich, I would have had a hard struggle to keep up, while he predicted a bright future for me at Sandhurst. He was right as I gained a Cadet Scholarship in my second term, £60 down, won the Modern History Prize and passed out fifteenth. I entered Sandhurst in September 1932.

CHAPTER II

Sandhurst – 1932–33

Mainly about my life as Gentleman Cadet

MANY HAVE ASKED why the Cadet College was called Sandhurst when the town at its gates and its postal address are Camberley. The original College building, however, stands in the Parish of Sandhurst in the County of Berkshire and at that time, the early years of the nineteenth century, Camberley as a town did not exist. In fact, until the Army arrived in the area after the Crimean War, there was no town between Farnham and Bagshot. For the geographically minded, the Berkshire–Surrey boundary runs from a three county point – Surrey, Berkshire and Hampshire – at the Blackwater Bridge, east for a short distance along the A30, and then takes a north easterly course across the Sandhurst Lake and on to the heathland behind the College. This puts the Old and New Buildings of my day, the Riding Schools, Gymnasium, Hospital and other ancillary buildings in Berkshire, but the original Officers' quarters by the London road, the Yorktown Gate, the post second war Victory College and Headquarters Office are in Surrey. This was academic in my day as neither the Staff nor the Cadets ever used the name 'Sandhurst' – to us it was always the 'RMC'.

The RMC was an anomaly. In the first place the Cadets were not soldiers given the status of Cadets, but Gentlemen Cadets, wearing the King's uniform, but as civilians – further, not only were they not paid, but their parents had to pay for them to be there. As I remember it, the full fees were £100 a term for three terms, with a further contingency payment of £70 in the first term and (I think) £20 in the last for uniform and kit. There were a number of reductions: King's Cadets and King's Indian Cadets, the sons of Officers of the British and Indian Armies killed in action, received large reductions. Any parent, particularly those who had served as Officers in the Great

War, could, on disclosure of his income, be considered for a reduction both in the fees and in the contingency payment. My father got a substantial reduction, which, together with my Prize Cadetship, Cadet Scholarship and Modern History Prize, a £12 Voucher on Wilkinson Sword, eased his burden considerably.

Much of the uniform and other kit issued and paid for by your parent's contingency allowance was not only of excellent quality but could be worn after commissioning; among these were the three pairs of boots, the long greatcoat and the blue patrols, together with the sports gear. Unfortunately, the ordinary drill uniform of a jacket and plus fours, while of officer's pattern, was made of coarse khaki serge of the same type as that used for other ranks' uniforms. No regiment would have allowed a new officer to wear it.

The strength of the College was four companies of about one hundred and fifty Gentlemen Cadets each, comprising juniors, intermediates and seniors. The Commandant was a Major General, with two Colonels as Chief Instructors for military and educational subjects respectively; they, together with the most formidable figure on the Staff, the Adjutant, usually a Guards Officer, formed the Headquarters. The four Companies were commanded by Majors, assisted by a Captain and two or three Subalterns. There were usually at least two Indian Army Officers and a French Officer attached and a number of Royal Army Education Corps Officers teaching specialized subjects, together with a large administrative staff headed by the Quartermaster. I think that all the Captains and above had served in the Great War and many of the Subalterns had only just missed it. The Warrant Officer and NCO Instructors were headed by the Battalion Sergeant Major, an RSM from the Foot Guards, known as the BSM or 'Bosom'. He and the Bandmaster were the only members of the staff to wear the RMC uniform, all others wearing their regimental badges and buttons. Each Company had a staff of a Company Sergeant Major and a Sergeant from the Guards and a Company Quartermaster Sergeant and a Sergeant from the Line. Nos 1 and 3 Companies were housed in the New Building, built after the South African War and 4 and 5 in the original Old Building. There was no No 2 Company; this had gone in one of the reorganizations after the Great War.

I reported to No 4 Company Office to be interviewed by the
Company Senior Under Officer, having duly digested a mass of
instructions and standing orders, including one telling me to arrive in
a sports coat and grey flannels with a 'gor blimey' cap. I marched in, as
I thought smartly, to be greeted by: 'What the hell do you mean by
slouching in like that? Get out and come in properly, swinging your
arms.' This was the usual treatment meted out to juniors, so that they
knew their place in RMC society. I remember at at the beginning of
my senior term, my section commander and I saw a junior reading
the company notice board with his hands in his pockets. We both
rushed up to him shouting, 'What the hell do you think you are
doing? Get your hands out of your pockets and stand up straight.' He
turned round and to my amazement I realized that it was one
Drybrough-Smith, who had been a Prefect in my House at Malvern,
of whom, at that time, I had had a great dread. He had come to
Sandhurst from the ranks and, regrettably, later was returned to his
unit, the 60th Rifles. He behaved with great gallantry during the siege
of Calais in 1940, winning a DCM before becoming a prisoner in
Germany.

While it was intended that juniors should be made to know their
place, there was none of the bullying that went on at West Point and
other military Academies – in fact, my son, in 1972, found Sandhurst
considerably tougher than in my day. The reason was that at this time
over 90 per cent of the GCs had learnt discipline in their Public
Schools and the remainder were from the ranks. Senior Under
Officers were allowed to award 'puttee parades' to anyone who was
really troublesome; these were so infrequent in my company that I
cannot remember much about them. They involved having to change
into working uniform with boots and puttees after dinner for extra
drill. The senior, irrespective of rank, at least in 4 Company, was
privileged; junior and intermediate Lance Corporals and Corporals
had no real command over senior GCs, only over those of their own
term. I remember once when, as a senior, I was taking a shower when
'Stand to your Rooms' – evening roll call – was announced. I was
wandering back to my room, when I saw the Orderly Corporal, a
junior, looking into my room, and being admonished by a senior
Corporal: 'you always report seniors present whether they are or not.'

4 Company had a public school sort of privilege – a junior, irrespective of rank, was forbidden to pass through a doorway in front of a senior; most seniors seeing a junior looking over his shoulder would wave him on, but woe betide him if he did not stop and look.

There is no doubt that juniors were worked extremely hard for the first six weeks; until the junior drill competition when they 'passed off the square' and were deemed fit to parade with other GCs; then came a long weekend's leave followed by their reward – four very easy weeks with very little drill, so little indeed, that on several days in the week, they could parade in slacks instead of boots and puttees. In my time all juniors had to compete in the junior boxing competition, whether they were experienced or not – although there were separate classes for beginners and experienced. To get them fit, the wretched juniors were herded out to run round the lakes before breakfast. Juniors paraded for the first day or two in 'civvies' – the sports coat and flannels with the gor blimey cap that we had been ordered to bring. The bulk of our kit was then issued, except for our uniform jackets and plus fours which were being made to measure. Until these had passed the eagle eye of the Adjutant, juniors paraded in brown dungarees with uniform cap and boots and puttees. One of the tabloids got hold of a picture of a junior squad practising the slow march and published it with the caption: 'Who are these – convicts?' There was trouble in my senior term – the small local tailoring firm lost the contract, which was awarded to the large firm which contracted for other ranks' uniform. They were unable to satisfy the Adjutant as late as the junior drill competition so no marks were awarded for turn out and the uniforms were scrapped and replaced by new ones made by the original firm.

A drill period was something not to be forgotten – fifty minutes being chased by four staff NCOs, without even a 'Stand at Ease', much less a 'Stand Easy'. I will always remember my first time 'on the square' – I thought I must be in a madhouse. There was CSM Cobb, barking orders, with Sergeant Shimmans screaming on one flank and the little Royal Scots CQMS on the other, and the star turn, Sergeant Brown of the Welch Regiment, marching backwards as fast as we did forwards, beating time with his pacestick and screaming 'epp – doit, epp – doit' (left-right) at the top of his voice. There were certain rules for the staff in dealing with the GCs – they must always address them as 'Mr' or 'Sir' and collectively as 'Gentlemen'; they were not supposed to strike them with their pacesticks – although a tap on the shoulder with a bellow: 'Stand up straight Mr Mains, Sir' was allowed. Some of the phrases used were hallowed by time – 'dancing about like lot of Victoria Girls' and 'standing like Venus on a rock cake' were two of CSM Cobb's. The use of 'Mr' was so ingrained that one GC in my time was addressed as 'Mr the Duke of Roxburgh'. I had difficulty in numbering off at the speed required so I took refuge in the rear rank. This provoked: 'I see you in the rear rank Mr Mains, Sir!' or 'The idlest gentleman that I have ever seen on this square, Mr Mains, Sir, a typical rear rank man.'

For convenience all staff NCOs were addressed as 'Staff' irrespective of rank, with the exception of the BSM who was 'Sir'. He, Mr Dobson, used to ride around majestically on a bicycle, and on seeing a number of Cadets would boom, 'Good morning, Gentlemen.' It was inevitable that some junior would answer, 'Good morning, Staff,' at which he would dismount, throw his bicycle to the ground, rush up to the offender and bellow, 'I call you Sir, you call me me Sir,' and rising to a crescendo, 'Do you understand – Sir?', punctuating with taps on the offender's chest with his stick.

GCs were fed and accommodated much the same as junior officers with one exception; while you had the share of a servant who did your room and cleaned your buttons, it was a serious offence if he cleaned your leather, rifle or bayonet. Juniors were confined to the College for their first few weeks, actually until their leather came up to the standard required by the platoon Under Officer. This entailed the endless polishing of boots' toecaps, belts, and bayonet frog, and the burnishing of the hilt of the bayonet, the rifle's bolt and backsight. I nearly got into trouble over my rifle – it was explained that I must strip all the wood off the barrel to remove any traces of the grease which had been put on the metal as a preservative. In doing this I inadvertently broke off a small piece of wood beside the backsight; however, as it was very small, a judicious application of brown boot polish concealed the break. Rifles were handed in at the end of term and another drawn on returning for the next term; this had been copiously regreased before re-issue. I got the hang of this chore in my senior term – I merely took the rifle to the showers and ran scalding hot water down it; this flushed out the grease. I do not suppose it did the rifle much good but that was not my worry. Juniors were given a respite from the after dinner leather inspections for the last few weeks of their first term but less frequent inspections started again in the intermediate term. Seniors were seldom required to 'show their leather', particularly those in junior platoons, and the prohibition against servants cleaning your leather was largely relaxed. My family lived at Chiswick, so I went home every Saturday after Adjutant's Parade and paid my servant half a crown to do my Sam Browne belt for Sunday's Church Parade.

Although each company was divided into platoons and sections, the only time that the company paraded as such was for the before breakfast inspection, the so called 'shaving parade'; few cadets had to shave but each platoon Under Officer made a meticulous dress inspection, and the slightest bit of fluff meant your name being taken. GCs were marched by terms to work on foot or on bicycles, and to provide commanders for the juniors, one of them was nominated each week by the CSM as the ICJ (in charge juniors). 'On passing off the square', some four juniors were promoted Lance Corporals – they would normally become Corporals in their intermediate term, and Under Officers in their senior. Of the four platoons, two were composed of juniors and two of mixed intermediates and seniors, each having a senior as platoon commander and platoon sergeant. Copying the system in the Guards (Training) Depot, each junior section had a senior Corporal as section commander with a senior GC to assist him – the 'trained soldier' in Guards parlance. The shortness of the course meant that there was little time to assess GCs' capabilities properly, and there is no doubt that mistakes were made. The Senior Under Officer in my intermediate term was a disaster – he was not sure of himself and was in the state described as 'windy'. It was unfortunate that CSM Cobb had left and his number two, Sergeant Shimmans, appointed CSM; he was even more windy than the SUO. It was usual for the Company to parade some twenty minutes before it was due on a Battalion parade; but our SUO, to be on the safe side, would make it thirty minutes. On top of this Shimmans would be rampaging about the passages earlier still, screaming at the SUO: 'Mr X, Sir, why is the Company not on parade?' This put us all on edge. It was a great joy that the incumbent in my senior term, Bill Gore-Langton, an old Etonian, while not a 'ball of fire', was completely unflappable and a very nice person, under whom the company soon settled down; Shimmans, I am glad to say, had been found wanting and returned to his unit.

In my own case, I made a slow start and did not shine, except in academic work, which I found ridiculously easy; in fact in my junior term, I got 99 per cent in a military geography paper and was nearly accused of cheating. I was average at drill, rather below average at PT and, although coming on fast, I was in the beginners' ride in the riding school, not having ridden since I was eight, and these were the subjects that counted. However I got on well with the Company staff, who looked upon me as a reasonable being who gave them no trouble.

The result was that I failed to get a stripe in my senior term, but I did get the trained soldier position. My experience in rugger now came to the fore; in the ordinary course of events I would have merited a place in the scrum of the Company's A team, but as 4 Company had an above average number of good players, Bill Gore-Langton decided to try for the special Cup awarded for winning all three, A, B, and C competitions, by equalizing our three teams and I was selected to captain the C team. Bill's strategy paid off and we did the hat trick. This put me on a different footing and about one third into the term the CSM told me that I should have been a Corporal instead of one who was proving no good, but that there was no way of putting me up unless the other committed some offence and was 'broken'. Probably thanks to his advice to our Company Commander at the end of term, I got a bonus in the number of Company Commander's marks that I was awarded. These marks, maximum 250, were given for a GC's behaviour and general deportment; in 4 Company they were stereotyped – SUO 240 – JUOs 220 – Senior Sergeant (Cadet CSM) 200 – Sergeants 180 – Corporals 160 etc; to my amazement I found I had received 200.

I remember little about the Officer Instructors – the Commandant, Sir Reginald May, did not continue in the service; the Adjutant, Norman Gwatkin, commanded a Guards Brigade at the end of the

War, and then held a post in the Royal Household. I remember the two Indian Army Officers, Captain Sangster of the Frontier Force, whose lugubrious expression and taciturn manner led him to be called 'Happy Gangster', the other, Captain Carroll, Baluch Regiment, notable for his flamboyant mess dress, rifle green jacket with scarlet piping and cherry pink overalls. My Company Commander was 'Old Nick', Major Nicholson, 16th/5th Lancers, a wealthy cavalry officer connected with Nicholson's Gin. That he was a good soldier was not in doubt, this was shown by his later heroic defence of Calais in 1940; but we hardly ever saw him. He did not interview juniors individually on their arrival but greeted them collectively in the anteroom with a few sharp sentences. I only once spoke to him; that was when I was charged with 'idle on parade'. Another GC had inadvertently knocked my rifle out of my hand. Then it was 'won't drill in the Government's time, drill in your own time – one extra drill, march out'. Also in 4 Company was a Lieutenant Orgill of the Manchester Regiment, known as 'Bogwheel' (bicycle), who interviewed me as a prospective officer of the Worcestershire Regiment as he was looking after their interests. Shortly after I left many of the RAEC Officers were sent to the new Indian Military Academy, where I met them again as I was posted to the 2/9th Gurkhas in the same station. There was Major Cole, whose book *Imperial Military Geography* was the standard work at the time; unfortunately the War proved his theories to be complete fallacies, especially as regards Singapore and the Far East. Others were Captain Kirkwood, reputed to be the oldest Captain in the British Army, and Captain Lunt, the father of General James Lunt, the military historian and author. My favourite was the Major, whose name I have forgotten, who taught modern history; this was not because he awarded me the Modern History Prize, but because he was incapable of running the full course of three evening instructional periods; after a a few minutes into the second period, he would dismiss the class to 'private study', the actual study consisting of a leisurely bath and changing into patrols for dinner in Mess.

There were only two GCs, about my time, who achieved fame, both of whom joined Gurkha Regiments. One was General Sir Walter Walker, 8th Gurkhas, of Malayan jungle warfare fame and the other the author John Masters, 4th Gurkhas. There were a few of the nobility and sons of wealthy parents, but the bulk of the GCs were from what is now called upper middle class with a large proportion from Army families. My senior term platoon Commander was Heathcote-Amery, of the Devonshire family, and the platoon Sergeant a rather tough A Cadet called Bury; my section commander was Fairweather, later a 4th Gurkha, who was tragically shot down by the Germans at Habbaniya while attached to the RAF. As Fairweather was a boxing 'Blue', he was usually absent at practice after dinner, so it fell to me to attend at the juniors' leather inspection with a book to record my seniors' remarks. This was worth a guinea a minute as the language of both Heathcote-Amery and Bury was spectacular. They would let fly at any junior whom they thought idle: 'F— awful boot,' and whang, it was chucked into a corner; B— idle belt,' and off that went into another corner. I was so helpless with laughter that often I did not get down their remarks, when they would turn on me and remind me that I was not there to laugh but to record what they said.

My term was the last to admit Indian Cadets as the Indian Military Academy had now opened. There were three in 4 Company. Nawabzada (Crown Prince) Salim Khan came from a small princely State near Bombay; he left the Army after a few years. The other two were my friends – Mohammad Usman from Lucknow and Pran Nath Narang from Lahore. Usman joined the Baluch Regiment and at Partition opted for India; he was killed as a Brigadier on the Indian side in Kashmir. Narang was attached with me to the Dorsets and then joined the Frontier Force Regiment – he was killed in Burma.

CHAPTER III

Sandhurst (*continued*)

Mainly about Sandhurst

SANDHURST WAS A very close knit community – all coming from the same background, the British Public School; even a number of the Army Cadets were from these schools. We were all, again except for the A Cadets, of the same age and, indeed very young – in our nineteenth or twentieth year; thus it was a very conservative body to whom Communists, and even the Labour Party, were anathema. We were proud that we were joining the King's Army – I remember one Instructor telling us that we belonged to the King and not to Parliament or any political body; in fact, at that time, King George V took a very great interest in 'his Army' and had to be consulted and approve any changes. We were inward looking, knowing that we were the best without any advertisement. There was no Sovereign's Parade, only a low-key Passing Out Parade with the salute taken by a senior military figure, usually the Chief of the Imperial General Staff; the Adjutant did ride up the steps of the Old Building however. There was no immediate wearing of an officer's uniform or insignia; we went home as civilians after the Parade to be commissioned at a later date. My term passed out about 20th December 1933, but we were not commissioned until 1st February 1934. There was a story recounted with pride that King George V had said that he wished that his Guards would drill as well as we did. During the whole of my time, however hot the weather, no GC fainted on parade, not even during the presentation of new Colours by the Duke of Connaught when the temperature on the day, and indeed during rehearsals, approached 90°F and we wore flannel shirts, heavy serge uniforms with puttees and boots and brown leather gloves. No one fell out – we just would not have dared; not only would we have been on a charge of 'inattention on parade' but the stigma would have remained for the whole of our service.

As we had not achieved our twenty first birthdays, the College was *in loco parentis* and this produced some restrictions which would be unheard of today. No GC could bring a private car to Sandhurst and, in addition, he was forbidden even to drive one except during the vacation, Easter recess or a long weekend granted to the whole College. GCs could buy a bottle of beer at lunch and a glass of port at dinner, which was obligatory on the weekly band night, to drink the King's health. The effect of alcohol on Cadets varied considerably – those like myself who had been allowed by our parents to have wine and beer in moderation during our school holidays were unlikely to get into trouble, but those who were unused to drinking were in a different category. On returning from day leave on Saturdays and Sundays one had to sign in in front of the Duty Officer, then stand to attention and say 'good night, Sir', turn about and march out. If you could do this, you had passed the sobriety test. There was no prohibition against smoking off duty; in fact, Rothmans and Weinbergs produced special Virginian and Turkish cigarettes with the RMC badge on them.

There were four punishments which could be meted out to Cadets – Company Commanders could award one or more extra drills, a sixty-minute period of drill in the afternoon free time – and by the Commandant, restrictions, rustication or finally expulsion. Restriction meant that the recipient was confined to the College grounds, had to wear uniform at all times, do extra drills and answer his name, properly dressed, whenever the defaulters call was blown. Rustication and expulsion required the Cadet to leave the College, for ever when expelled, but when rusticated he could rejoin at the next term, but had to do the previous term again.

The College routine was not unlike that of a school – Reveille at 7, then 'shaving parade', followed by breakfast. This was taken in the clothes appropriate for the first instructional period – drill, riding or PT Order; in PT Order the College red and white blazer and white flannels were worn over the PT singlet and blue shorts with the College scarf and the Victorian red and white pillbox cap. Monday to Friday, instructional periods were from 9 am to lunch at 1 pm; the drill, riding and PT periods were invariably in the morning. Very little time was given between periods for moving from one venue to another or to change clothes; one particularly difficult move was in the intermediate term: PT to Riding which involved a mad scramble, pulling off singlet and shorts – on with shirt, collar and tie, woe betide if you had mislaid your collar studs, then breeches, ankle boots and leggings, and then out again at the double for inspection before marching to the riding schools. Between lunch and tea was free time, there were no compulsory games, followed by classes until 7 pm, except on Wednesday which was a half holiday. Then change into patrols for dinner at 7.30 – 'rooms' (roll call) at 10 and lights out at 10.15. Saturday was Adjutant's parade which usually finished about 10.15, dependent on the Adjutant's mood and what he thought of the parade's drill, and Sunday was Church Parade ending about noon. On these days, provided you had entered your name on the leave sheet and it had not been deleted for some misdemeanour, you were free and could leave the College until 10 pm.

There were two vacations of about eight weeks each, from late December to early February and during July and August, with a two weeks Easter recess; three long weekends were granted to the whole college – one in November and the other two in March and May; these were the only leaves which were granted to juniors. Weekend leaves were granted to the others as a privilege – one in the autumn term and two in the spring–summer term. I found, however, that if you stood in well with the Staff you could probably wangle an extra one in your senior term, as old Nick would sanction any leave application backed by the CSM. I certainly got one – I went to company office and the following conversation ensued:

'I think that I would like leave this weekend, Staff.'

'You have had one weekend already, Mr Mains, Sir.'

'I know, Staff, but I think I could do with another.'

A grin and 'You put in an application, Sir, and I will see what I can do.'

There were one or two extra leaves and holidays – Derby Day was a holiday with late leave. My Company hired a double-decker bus to take us to Epsom, then up to London and back to the RMC, leaving at midnight; my father wished to take me to dinner and a theatre so after the race, I went up to Town by train, and later joined the returning bus. Hunting leave was very generously given; some of the

wealthier GCs kept horses at livery nearby and it was possible for the
top ride to hire government horses; in fact, hunting was looked upon
almost as duty. There was no evening roll call on the last night of
term; you could stay out all night provided you were present and
sober for the Passing Out Parade.

The Author John Masters, who was a contemporary of mine, wrote
at some length in *Bugles and a Tiger* of riotous behaviour by Cadets
during his time, but I can remember only one major incident in this
period. A new Commandant and Adjutant had arrived not long
before I joined and it was thought that they had been appointed to
tighten up discipline. The Commandant, 'Reggie' (Sir Reginald)
May, was commonly thought of as a 'Bible Puncher', and the
Adjutant, Norman Gwatkin, was far removed from the flamboyant
character of his predecessor, 'Boy' Browning. Many of the incidents,
mainly on the last night of term, were harmless pranks, which,
provided that they were within the College grounds and did not get
into the Press, did little harm. However one exploit before my time
was the blocking of the main London road by the guns from the Old
Building Square, which did get into the papers, and it was strongly
rumoured that, also before my time, some GCs had taken part in Sir
Oswald Mosely's Blackshirt Rallies in London's East End.

At the end of my junior term the only incident was putting the
guns into the lake; I remember this as 4 Company was roused out at
6 am on a cold December morning to pull them out. I do not think
that there was any trouble in my intermediate term, but a serious riot
in my senior. There had been a spate of petty thefts in 4 Company in
the summer; no culprit was found but one of the servants was
suspected. The work of a certain junior was not up to scratch and he
'dropped' that term; this meant that he was transferred to a New
Building Company, I think it was 1, where he had to do his junior
term again. The thefts started in this company and later he was caught
red handed stealing a fountain pen. The Commandant, possibly to
spare his parents – his father was a distinguished officer and Deputy
Governor of the Tower of London – did not expel him but punished
him by 'restrictions' for the remainder of the term. On hearing this,
his new company rose up in wrath and proceeded to 'lake' him; this
involved stripping him naked, covering him with boot polish and

then carrying him down to the lake and throwing him in. The whole of his company and many of the other New Building company joined in, and naturally there was a good deal of noise, shouting and blowing of hunting horns, which attracted the attention of Lieutenant Heard, the map reading instructor. He attempted to intervene and got pushed in himself. All this was bad enough, but the papers made a great deal of it, including an interview with the culprit's father; he made matters worse by saying that while his son had got what he deserved, he deprecated the fact that two of the ring leaders were sprigs of the nobility who were little better. He was referring to two Peers who used to spend much of their time on 'restrictions'. There was a strong rumour that owing to 'cuts' in the Armed Forces, some senior Cadets might not be commissioned at the end of term but would be sent home to await a vacancy. The authorities let it be known that if there was any trouble at the end of term they would know who would be deferred. There was no trouble.

Security as is now known did not exist. The RMC grounds were open to the public, and were used by the citizens of Camberley as their public park. Rifles were not locked up, but stood in a rack in each Cadet's room which were not locked – each room did have a small fixed strong box for money and valuables. There were no armed sentries and the only security force was a small number of elderly War Department Constabulary, known to the Cadets as 'blue bottles'. They were not particularly popular as one of their main tasks was the recovery of GCs' bicycles left about the place and not returned to the cycle shed in the evening, for which the owner was fined. A Constable wheeling in a bicycle would be greeted with shouts of 'lovely bottle'. The 'borrowing' of bicycles and cycle lamps and leaving them anywhere in the College grounds was not considered by the Cadets as stealing, so on a visit to the cinema in Camberley, you locked your cycle and took the lamp in with you.

Finally, what did the RMC do to fit me to hold a Commission? In some respects very little; during the twenties, the curriculum lurched between turning out a trained soldier, a trained officer, an educated gentleman or some combination of all three. When I joined the last had just come into the ascendancy – the new educational policy as it was called. The general idea was that while keeping the sacred cows of Drill, Equitation and PT, a university type of education should prevail. The theoretical training, therefore, was military history and geography, the study of military campaigns in a general sense, the organization of the Army again in a very general sense, and a certain amount of what now might be called civics – we had the intricacies of the organization of labour, unemployment benefit and so on explained to us. This latter study was a popular subject as it involved visits by coach to factories – I remember that my term went on a day long visit to the Morris factory at Cowley. I regret that some of the more right wing GCs called the earnest RAEC Captain, who organized it, a Communist. There was no form of tactical training whatsoever nor any instruction in how to fire or maintain any weapon, nor to command a platoon in barracks. The idea was to teach the Cadets how to think rather than how to do. It was thought that detailed military training would be better taught in the Regimental Depots after commissioning. This was particularly hard on those GCs going to the Indian Army who did not go to a Depot but straight to an attachment with an Infantry Battalion in India and were given command of a platoon immediately on joining. During field training, I found the knowledge of tactics that I had acquired in the OTC of more value than any Sandhurst training.

The above might seem to imply that I did not enjoy my time at the RMC and it was all a waste of time – far from it; it was a wonderful transition from schoolboy to grown man, probably in this respect better than University, as it was a transition with discipline. I certainly enjoyed my time, even my junior term, as all along there was a sense of achievement. We had a great sense of pride in belonging to an institution which through the years had been a model for other countries and to an Army which then and now in its disciplined behaviour in many and varied tasks was and is still second to none.

CHAPTER IV

Unattached List Indian Army – 1934

Attached to the 1st Battalion The Dorsetshire Regiment

IT WOULD BE LOGICAL to suppose that the criteria for posting newly commissioned officers to regiments would be first, the candidate's suitability, and the second, his choice – but, in fact, the first had very little to do with it, the actual first being money, linked to regimental selection; the finest rider in the world would have had no chance of joining a cavalry regiment, unless he had a sufficient private income to maintain the regiment's standard of living.

Selection was very much in the hands of Regiments rather than the War Office and could be summarised – a large private income was necessary for the Household Brigade, the Cavalry, Highland Regiments, most Rifle Regiments, particularly the 60th Rifles and the Rifle Brigade, and a few other Infantry Regiments, notably the 43rd and 52nd Light Infantry; there was no doubt that many other regiments preferred a candidate with some private means. No private means were required for posting to the Indian Army, and selection would come later after the obligatory one year attachment to a British Regiment. A curious facet was that no Cadet was commissioned direct into two most important Corps, the Royal Army Service Corps or the Royal Army Ordnance Corps – these were officered by transfers from Cavalry and Infantry for the former and from the Royal Artillery for the latter. There were few enthusiastic candidates; as these Corps qualified for extra pay, many officers transferred for purely financial reasons, such as debt or a youthful marriage, and some regrettably were plain 'throw outs' from their original regiments.

Promotion in cavalry and infantry was by vacancy, thus in regiments where many officers only served for a short period as a social 'cachet', a captaincy could be achieved in about six years, in those which attracted the sons of the landed gentry, ten to twelve years was nearer the mark, but in the ordinary 'county' regiment where the average officer joined to serve until he had gained his pension, twelve to fifteen was the norm; indeed, in 1934 there was at least one subaltern who had served in the Great War.

My father was prepared to give me an allowance of £60 per annum, which, of course, left me with the choice of an English county regiment. I had no family connections but I had been a member of the Malvern College OTC, which was affiliated to the Worcestershire Regiment. It so happened that the Inspecting Officer for Malvern OTC's annual inspection in my last term was Field Marshal Sir Claude Jacob, the Colonel of that Regiment, and I had been introduced to him during the inspection. During my intermediate term, I was told by Lieutenant 'Bogwheel' Orgill that I was a certainty for a vacancy. However in my senior term I began to have doubts – the idea of inspecting my platoon's feet for some fifteen years or so was not an exciting one. I learnt that things were very different in the Indian Army – time scale promotion, nine years for a captaincy and seventeen for a majority. In addition Indian Army Officers did not command platoons, but on joining were 'company officers' and with the usual paucity of officers were quite likely to be commanding a company, irrespective of rank, very soon after joining. Another inducement was the possibility of a secondment to a Frontier Corps, the Assam Rifles, or the Burma Frontier Force to break the monotony of regimental service. The only drawback was the possible loss of career if Indianization of the Officer Corps was speeded up but this appeared to be in the then distant future, so, somewhat to the annoyance of Orgill, I switched and put in my preference for the Indian Army.

I did not have to make up my mind as to choice of a Regiment as Cadets were not commissioned direct into Indian Regiments but into a holding Corps, the Unattached List Indian Army (ULIA) and sent out to India to serve for a year attached to a British Regiment. Newly commissioned officers, thus, had a chance to learn the language of their future soldiers and absorb the atmosphere and customs of India.

Most of those going to the Indian Army had some family connections and many were assured of a posting to the 'family regiment' even before leaving the RMC. I had no such connections

HMT Nevasa, 1934.

but one advantage – my Father's allowance would enable me to apply for any regiment, including cavalry, which was what I wanted. I therefore put in for an attachment to the 1st Battalion of the Dorsetshire Regiment, stationed at Sialkot in the Punjab, as this was the Headquarters of the 2nd Cavalry Brigade and two cavalry regiments, one British and one Indian, were stationed there.

My preference was acceded to and I was ordered to report at Southampton on 16th February for embarkation on HMT (His Majesty's Transport) *Nevasa*. The *Nevasa*, a coal burning liner of 9,000 tons, was owned and staffed by the British India Line, a subsidiary of the P & O: ships on permanent charter to the War Office did not wear their company livery, but were painted white with yellow funnels and a broad blue stripe round the hull. Officers and their families travelled first class in the same luxury as in any comparable liner, WOs and Sergeants second and soldiers' families, but not the husbands, third class. Soldiers travelled 'troop deck', that is in hammocks slung in what had been the holds. The senior officer travelling was designated 'OC Troops' and was assisted by a permanent staff of an RSM with provost and clerical personnel. The navigation and general running of the ship was entirely in the hands of the civilian officers and crew.

We, the ULIAs, numbering about thirty, had no troops to look after, so our voyage was little different from a passage on an ordinary liner; further, on application to the ship's RSM, the four of us sharing a cabin were allotted a soldier as a batman to clean our buttons and shoes – we wore uniform until lunch and mess dress for dinner. Ours was a fast voyage calling only at Port Said to coal, which was a pity as we missed going ashore at such places as Gibraltar, Malta and Aden. Port Said was the changeover point as regards uniform, changing from ordinary to tropical – this necessitated a visit to the ship's 'wanted on voyage' baggage room to get out our khaki drill and white mess dress. A visit to Simon Arz's famous store was obligatory to buy our civilian sun helmets, the well known 'Bombay Bowlers'. I had time, also, to take a taxi to visit my mother's grave, which was then still in excellent condition.

The passage down the Red Sea in February was passable; of course, the ship was not air conditioned, nor had it the more modern 'blowers' but only electric fans. There were also wind scoops; those for the cabins were of metal which fitted into the portholes and to ventilate the troop decks were canvas scoops rigged to the masts; in both cases the openings were turned towards the direction of travel. Some of us thought that we needed exercise, so we persuaded the Chief Engineer to allow us to do a two hour trick in the stokehold, much to the amusement of the Pathan stokers. I had forgotten about this, until almost at the end of my service, an Indian Brigadier said to me, 'Tony, do you remember how we stoked the boilers of the *Nevasa* in the Red Sea?' This officer was then 2nd Lieutenant 'Kay' Kumaramangalam, later to become the Chief of the Army Staff. He was one of the two Indian Officers on this voyage; the other was Pilot Officer Engineer, who later became an Air Marshal.

We arrived at Alexandra Dock, Bombay one morning in early March; it so happened that the two other officers who were being attached to the Dorsets were also from 4 Company, Harper and Evan Rowland Jones. Both had been born in India and Evan had been partly educated in the country at the Lawrence Military School at Mount Abu before coming home at sixteen to go to an English Public School, Canford. Both, unlike me, knew which Indian Regiments they were likely to join – Harper to the 10th Gurkhas and Evan RJ to the 11th Sikhs. A fourth officer from 4 Company was also coming to the Dorsets, Pran Nath Narang, the son of a Minister in the Punjab Government. He had gone ahead and he would join us at Sialkot. The Embarkation Staff came aboard to arrange our dispersal and the three of us for Sialkot were to travel that evening on the Frontier Mail to Wazirabad Junction, where, on the third morning, we would change into a local train for the final two hour run to Sialkot. A special portion of the Mail was to start from the adjacent Ballard Pier Station to save the military passengers the trouble of joining the train at Bombay Central. With the Embarkation Staff came the servants (bearers) whom the Regiment had selected and sent down to meet us. Mine, Mohammed Ishaque, relieved me of my hand luggage and my agents, Cooks, would clear the heavy baggage and book it on the Frontier Mail, so we were free to enjoy Bombay until the evening. For the railway minded, I have included as an Appendix, 'The First Indian Journey' from my book *Soldier with Railways*.

A great deal has been said and written about the reception and treatment of ULIAs by their respective British Regiments, much of it about the poor showing of the regiments concerned. As for us four, the first thing that the CO said was that we would be sent to companies where we would immediately be given command of a platoon, and that we would be treated exactly the same as the Regiment's subalterns. Further, if we were accepted by top flight regiments the Dorsets would consider this to their credit. There can be no doubt that treatment of ULIAs must have varied from regiment to regiment, but I have never been able to put my finger on any case of poor treatment. There is a story often told of a Guest Night when a visiting General saw some officers eating at a separate table and on enquiry was told, 'Oh, they are only those Indian Army chaps,' to which the General replied, 'Well, I am an Indian Army chap so I will go and sit with them,' – but I have never been able to nail the story. The position of Indian Officers could sometimes arise; Narang certainly had no cause for complaint. The Dorsets had had a Sikh officer attached just before us and many of the private soldiers still spoke highly of him – 'That Mr Singh, he was a proper gentleman,' was a remark that I heard. Indians trained at Sandhurst (and Woolwich) were designated King's Commissioned Indian Officers and held the same commissions as British Officers, in HM's Land Forces,

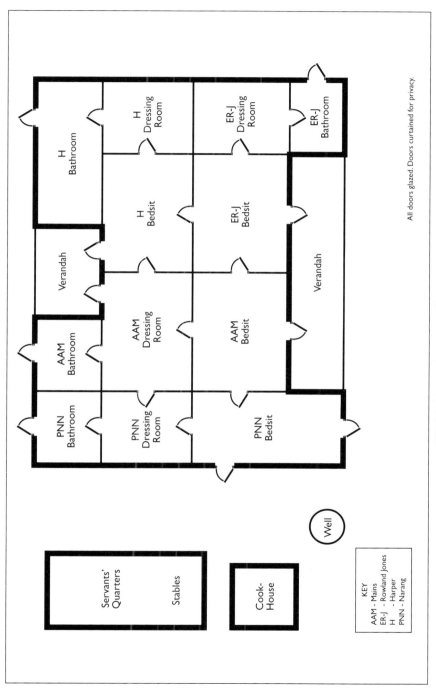

All doors glazed. Doors curtained for privacy.

KEY
AAM - Mains
ER-J - Rowland Jones
H - Harper
PNN - Narang

ULLA's bungalow – Sialkot 1934.

so they had power of command over British troops. My term was the last to have Indian Cadets as, in future, they were to be trained at the new Indian Military Academy at Dehra Dun – further, they would be granted commissions in HM's Indian Land Forces, which gave them no such power. This was not appreciated at first and in March 1935, the Dorsets received an Indian Christian officer, George Isaacs; he was sent to take over No 6 Platoon from me. We were in the middle of this when an urgent message was received from the Orderly Room to stop everything until Isaacs' position was clarified; the next day, however, came a signal that Indian Commissioned Officers had received a special dispensation from the Viceroy.

The four of us were quartered in a typical 'plains' bungalow in the Dorset's area of the cantonment. Sialkot like most cantonments had no government quarters for officers, so each officer in theory could make his own arrangements for accommodation and rent, pay the landlord direct and receive lodging allowance in lieu. In practice, however, Station HQ kept a tight hold, allotting certain bungalows to each regiment and browbeating the landlords into charging rents which equated to an officer's lodging allowance. Our bungalow, like most, could be used as a junior officer's married quarter as well as four single quarters. It was square and flat roofed with verandahs back and front. The four principal rooms each opened into each other, as well as onto the verandah and also to the ancillary rooms such as a study, pantries and bathrooms. It did not divide equally into four single quarters. I came off best, I cannot remember why, getting a principal room in front as my bedsit, another at the back as my dressing room and a bathroom. Evan and Harper each got a principal room as a bedsit, with a dressing room and bathroom adjacent at the side. Poor Narang, who arrived four days later, got what was left, the ancillary rooms on the other side, giving him a much smaller bedsit with a dressing room and bathroom. The rooms were furnished by a furniture contractor to whom we paid the hire. There was electricity but no piped water; in due course, we each bought a table fan for the hot weather and water was provided by the *bhisti*, who drew it from the well in the compound and filled the large earthenware pots (*chatties*) in the bathrooms. Sanitation was a commode in the bathroom, usually referred to as a 'thunderbox'; this was emptied periodically by the sweeper. We each had a bearer and we shared the wages of the *bhisti*, sweeper and the *dhobi* who washed our clothes.

Officers' domestic arrangements in India were entirely different from those pertaining in England, where they received free quarters, furniture and servants, as well as rations. To compensate, India had a consolidated pay structure which was supposed to take into account the Indian cost of living and an element for the cost of those amenities which were not provided free. The pay of a 2nd Lieutenant, therefore, was about Rs 360 (about £28) a month, about double the rate in the United Kingdom. Another anomaly was that while the UK paid in advance, India paid in arrears, which meant officers living on monthly credit.

We wore roughly the same uniform as the Dorsets, except for our own regimental badges and buttons – for everyday parades, khaki shorts and shirts with brown boots, hose tops and ankle puttees in the hot weather and British pattern barathea jacket and plus fours in the winter. Ceremonial dress, winter and summer, was a khaki drill jacket and breeches with long light coloured puttees; the Sam Browne belt was worn in all orders of dress with swords for ceremonial parades or when Orderly Officer. The Dorsets did not have any special field service equipment, wearing the SB belt with revolver, field glasses, haversack and waterbottle. We wore our Sandhurst patrols for dinner in the cold weather and white drill mess jackets and overalls in the summer.

The training year was universal for all regiments, British and Indian – individual training from March to the end of September, followed by field firing and collective training up to Christmas; January and February saw brigade training and every now and again large scale manoeuvres. Little outdoor training, however, could be carried out in most parts of India in August and September, the 'rainy season', and British regiments' training was further interrupted by the 'hill moves'. British personnel spent at least some of the hot season in the cool of the hill stations. The HQ and families went up in mid April and came down in late September; so as not to denude large areas of India of British troops, half of each unit only went up at a time, changing over in July. The Dorsets had two 'hill stations' in the Simla Hills, Solan for

Waterwheel in action at Sialkot.

the HQ and one company and Jutogh for the other. Evan and Harper went up with the first party, leaving Pran Nath and me for the second. The hot weather routine was parade at 6 am, or even 5.30 if the company was firing on the range, breakfast at 8 or 8.30, company office from 9 or 9.30 until lunch at 1 pm – siesta 2 to 4 – tea brought from the Mess by your bearer at 4, followed by an hour with the Munshi (language teacher), after which games or exercise – and finally dinner at 8.30, which was a parade, except on Thursdays and Sundays which were 'supper nights' when dinner jackets were worn and one could eat at any time between 8.30 and 9.30. The medical authorities, at that time, would not allow British troops to undertake any outdoor activity between 10 am and 5 pm in the hot season, so games and outdoor recreation had to take place in the evening. Thursday and Sundays were holidays – but Church Parade, on a rota, was roughly once a month, each company having to produce two officers and a specified number of men.

The organization of a British infantry battalion in India in 1934 was a Headquarters, three rifle companies, and a machine gun company – such things as anti-tank and mortar platoons were still in the distant future. The support weapons were one light machine gun per rifle platoon, still the obsolete Lewis gun carried on a mule, and sixteen

Vickers machine guns. A curiosity was that while the Lewis gun mule was led by a British soldier, the machine gun mules had Indian leaders. The difficulty of keeping British units up to strength, while there was a large surplus of Indians from the martial classes, led the Government of India to recruit them for British Infantry and the still horsed Royal Artillery; in RA units only the gun numbers and gun drivers were British. The Indian platoon's men were subject to the Indian Army Act and had the IA's nomenclature of ranks, but wore the Dorset's badges and buttons. The same reasoning decreed that many tasks carried out in Britain by British troops, such as cooks and storemen, could be as well performed by Indian civilians, the so called followers; they were changed over from outgoing to incoming units as required. In addition to these 'public' followers, there were a host of private followers: these were the regimental canteen contractor's staff who ran the canteen, supper room and shop, together with a number of others licensed by him – the fried egg man, who attended the mess rooms at breakfast time, the 'char and wads' (tea and buns) vendor and the barbers; many soldiers made a shaving contract, the barber shaving his client in bed often while still asleep before reveille.

I was given command of No 6 Platoon in B Company – luckily, in view of my inexperience, I had the best platoon sergeant in the company, Sergeant Spicer, a strict disciplinarian, although very unpopular with the other ranks. My section commanders were very average, and so were the men; none of them were from Dorset but had been recruited from the Midlands unemployed. I also had a comic, the platoon mule leader, who boasted that he could do anything with his mule, even to getting under the animal and reappearing between its front legs. Another character was an old soldier, one 'Enery' Stokes; in view of his long service, he was put in charge of the 'ET (Early Treatment) Room' – men who had been out with a woman had to report there to disinfect themselves; if they did not and caught VD, it was treated as a self inflicted injury. The post carried an unpaid Lance stripe, and after a while Enery appeared at company office asking for a transfer back to No 6 platoon as he wished to try for further promotion. This caused general amusement in the company and the Company Sergeant Major, Dutot, a Channel Islander and an excellent Warrant Officer, tried to dissuade him but he insisted. He was quite useless as an NCO in the platoon and only lasted a week or so before he was 'broken'.

The platoon tried to put it across me as a new and inexperienced officer, but went too far. One day I was giving some orders when I heard: 'Who the f — hell does he think he is?'; luckily I could identify the speaker so I called out, 'Sergeant Spicer, take that man's name' and ran him up before the company commander who remanded him for the CO's Orderly Room. The CO told him that it would have been bad enough to have spoken thus to a Dorset officer, but far worse to have used such language to one who was the Regiment's guest and gave him twenty-eight days CB. I had no further trouble and at the end of my year the platoon presented me with an inkstand. The Dorsets were a good county regiment and as efficient as any British battalion in India, but, in general, the British units in India could hardly be described as in a state of instant readiness for war. The senior officers were usually too old and the men too young and inexperienced; in addition, the Great War had left a massive promotion block and the financial stringency of the thirties had left its mark in both England and India. The monotony of peacetime routine in an enervating climate did little for the morale of the private soldier, but it says much for the spirit of these men that as soon as they were extricated from this routine, their morale improved. Men involved in operations on the North West Frontier, subjected to intense heat in summer and severe cold in winter, remained mentally alert and full of fighting spirit, but regrettably in Sialkot, the 'roll on my boat' attitude prevailed.

As I was the most junior, I got the job of company messing officer. The barracks in Sialkot were what were known as 'Cholera Barracks', built in the eighteen fifties or sixties. To minimise the risk of infection, each barrack block was built at a considerable distance from its neighbour, and was self contained with cookhouses, ablution and latrine blocks adjacent; there were no mess halls, the inner verandah of the main barrack being used in lieu. Thus each company ran its own messing. Basic foodstuffs were provided from the Supply Depot, but groceries were bought from the Canteen; these were paid for partly by a per capita allowance and partly by stoppages from the men's pay. Three meals were provided – a hot breakfast, midday dinner and a light supper, the last being omitted at weekends as, after pay day on Fridays, most men preferred to eat out either in the Canteen or in the Bazaar. Unfortunately for the company messing account, the medical authorities considered that to eat a hot and heavy meal in temperatures of 115°F was unhealthy; indeed many men were covered in 'prickly heat'. They suggested that the hot dinner be taken in the evening and a light meal of salads substituted at midday. This was disastrous for the messing account – the soldiers objected strongly to the midday salads, so the light meal had to be augmented, and at weekends the evening dinners were largely wasted as few men turned up to eat them. Luckily the onset of the cold weather allowed a return to the status quo ante.

The Dorset's CO, Thwaites, was typical of the period; he had finished the Great War as a Brigadier and now, sixteen years later, he was only a Lieutenant Colonel and probably lucky to be that. All the Majors and Captains had served in the War and the senior subaltern had only just missed it. There was little initiative left in most of them. One stood out, Darryl Stanier, who was a Brevet Major; he achieved fame later as the Senior British Officer in Colditz; another, with more energy than most, was my company commander, Bob Goff, who taught me a great deal. I only remember a few of the subalterns. The next door bungalow had a quartet, only a few years senior to us, 'Vicar' Meade, 'Skinny' Laugher, very fat, 'Porky' Ewens, very slim and Bobby Hamblin, who was also in B Company and was my bear leader. They were very kind to us and it was tragic that Porky Ewens, who was with me later on the Intelligence Staff of Burma Army, died of a ruptured appendix during the Retreat as there was no surgeon available to operate. There was an older subaltern, 'Hamish' James, who taught us the guest night trick of 'burning one's nose'. The trick was to anoint your nose with methylated spirit from the table cigarette lighter and set fire to it. Provided you extinguished the flame before all the meths was burnt, it was quite painless.

The CO's wife was considered a bit of a dragon and was alleged to have been behind the unfortunate episode of the subaltern who wished to get married. It was generally thought that officers could not normally get permission to marry until they were thirty. This was not so, no permission was necessary, but those who did so against their

CO's wishes could find themselves in trouble, as they would receive neither marriage allowance nor free married quarters and might well end up in financial difficulties; further, their CO could insist on the officer living in single quarters in Mess. In this particular case the subaltern concerned, who had seven or eight years service, was under transfer to the home battalion whose CO had no objection. Mrs CO however, prevailed on Thwaites to have the battalion boycott the wedding – no reception in the Mess, no regimental wedding present and only one or two officers attending the actual ceremony.

Sialkot was in fact three separate entities – the City, the Civil Lines and the Cantonment. The Civil Lines were adjacent to the City, but the Cantonment, for reasons of health and infection, was at a distance of two or three miles. Sialkot City was famous for its two major industries – bagpipes and sports gear, particularly cricket bats and hockey sticks. The main railway station was here on the branch line from Wazirabad Junction to a terminus at Jammu. The Civil Lines consisted of the Kutchery, the generic name for the District Magistrate's Office and Courts, the Superintendent of Police's Office, the Police Lines, Jail and Civil Hospital, with the residences of the various officials.

Sialkot Cantonment was typical of a military station situated on the north India plains, a rectangular gridiron of roads embracing the troop's barracks and officer's bungalows, with a bazaar attached. The municipal services – electricity, water and sanitation – were provided by the Military Engineering Service and the military Station Commander was responsible for them and for the administration generally. The long side of the rectangle of about two miles was from north to south; east to west was rather less than a mile. About half way down the eastern side was the Saddar Bazaar, the main shopping centre. The main north–south road, the Mall, was part of the main road to Kashmir and the winter capital of that State, Jammu, was only thirty miles distant at the commencement of the Himalayan foothills. Sialkot itself was on the heavily irrigated flat Punjab plain. The barrack areas were on the west side with the officers' bungalows and messes adjacent in the centre. The north end of the cantonment housed the Dorsets, the 13/18th Hussars, 'G' Battery (Mercers Troop) Royal Horse Artillery and the British Military Hospital; the Brigade

Parade Ground and the lines of the Indian Cavalry Regiment, Hodsons Horse, were in the centre with the 10th (Training) Battalions of the 12th Frontier Force and 16th Punjab Regiments and the Indian Military Hospital at the south end. Brigade HQ, the Club and the Garrison Church were somewhere in the middle. While the area was green and beautiful in the cold weather, during the summer, until the rains came, it was a dusty dreary place.

An unusual feature in the Cantonment was the Kashmir Residency with its large well kept compound. The capital of the State of Jammu and Kashmir for the greater part of the year was Srinagar where the main Residency was situated. The Maharaja's Government, however, moved to Jammu for the winter months, partly for political reasons and partly because of the intense cold of the Kashmir Valley. The normal practice would have been to site the winter Residency there, but as the Sialkot Cantonment was only thirty miles distant, the Government of India presumably for financial or security reasons decided on that place.

At this distance of time, I do not remember the officers of other regiments, although, following custom, we had to call on the other Messes, the Brigade Commander, and the married officers of the Dorsets; the last involved placing two cards in a box fixed to the bungalow's gate, but the new fashion of signing a visitors' book was prevalent for the Messes. Until this was done you were a 'no person' and would not receive any invitations. The cold weather season was practically over when we arrived, so there was little social life. We found however that two officers from 4 Company a year senior to us, Pat Massey and Billy Oakes, had just joined Hodsons Horse.

I bought a car from a Major Crystal of the 13/18th, later to be be a contemporary of Glubb Pasha as Commandant of the Trans Jordan Frontier Force – possibly a daring or foolhardy act, as up to then I had never driven. However without any formal instruction, merely some advice from my friends, I dared to drive down to the Police Office in the Civil Lines to obtain a driving licence. I was interviewed by an elderly Anglo-Indian Deputy Superintendent who said, 'I suppose I should give you a test – wait, how did you get here?' I replied, 'I drove here,' on which he issued a licence. As the car had a registration book, that was all the documentation required; no Indian Province had compulsory third party insurance, and few, including the Punjab, a car tax. My car was a two seater AC, vintage 1923, with a dicky behind which would seat two more. Much of the body was of wood which had become dessicated in the hot climate, but it was my pride and joy and, although mainly used for getting about in Cantonments, it managed, in the following winter, to take my friends and me to picnics in the foothills beyond Jammu. It was the custom in B company for the CSM to march the company to the Ranges and the officers to proceed there direct on their bicycles; motoring being more pleasant than bicycling, I drove to the Ranges, but this provoked Bob Goff's wrath. He obviously considered that this was slacking so I got a peremptory order that, in the future, I was to parade the company at 5.30 am and march it to the Ranges and, further, march it back to barracks at the conclusion of the firing.

Evan and Harper departed to the 'Hills' in late April, leaving Pran Nath and me to endure the hot weather − 115°F in the shade. Our bungalow had no overhead fans; we had to exist with the small table fans that we had bought ourselves. Most officers slept out of doors under a mosquito net in the hot weather, but I found that this did not suit me as the light of the moon kept me awake; so I slept indoors with the fan on. I also discovered that in most areas, if you slept under a fan, the malaria risk was very small, so I seldom used a mosquito net and never contracted malaria.

As Pran Nath's father was a Minister in the Punjab Government, he had contacts in the Punjab hierarchy; one such was Sialkot's District Magistrate, an Indian member of the ICS who invited us to spend the day at his bungalow, which had a private swimming pool. He also gave us a highly spiced curry and as a result I had a very disturbed night. I got no sympathy from my bearer, Ishaque, who told me bluntly that if I, a Sahib, went dining with Indians, and Hindus at that, I only got what I deserved.

A and C Companies returned in early August and it was time for B and D to leave for their respective hill stations, in the case of B Company to Solan. Two special trains were laid on for consecutive days, each consisting of three 'military cars' for the soldiers, one four wheeled I class for the officers, one four wheeled II class for WOs and sergeants, and a brake van and two goods vehicles for baggage. The journey was uneventful, but of considerable interest to me as a railway enthusiast. As the most junior officer, it was my duty to oversee the loading of the baggage – no sinecure when the wagon was all steel and the temperature was over 100°F. At our long halt at Amritsar, I was sent to get the 'No looting certificate' from the duty Assistant Station Master as, without it, any damage on the station for the last few weeks would have been charged to us.

Pran Nath did much better than I as regards hill stations: Jutogh lay at an altitude of 6,400 ft and was almost a suburb of Simla, while Solan might be described as cheap and nasty as its altitude was only 4,900 ft, almost on the 'mosquito line', and, further, while not experiencing the fierce heat of the plains, it did not have the glorious fresh feel of the higher stations. This was aggravated by the lack of electricity – no fans and lighting by hot and smelly petromax and hurricane lamps which officers had to provide themselves. A few miles down the road towards Simla was the Solan Brewery, which produced quite the nastiest beer of anywhere in the world, and also comparable whisky, gin and rum. I had one treat – Pran Nath on a holiday sent one of his father's cars to bring me up to Simla to have tea and later dinner at the Cecil Hotel.

There was one unpleasant chore – collecting the pay from the Treasury at Kasauli, some thirty miles away and on a very winding hill road. This was done in a hired taxi with an armed escort of two soldiers; even travelling on the front seat, I was often on the verge of being sick and, sometimes, we had to stop for one or other of the escort. I was amused when one day our medical officer, a Captain, announced his intention of coming to Kasauli with us, and was holding forth in the Mess how, as he would be sitting in front, he was unlikely to be sick. This annoyed one of the Dorset officers who told him bluntly that MOs were non combatants and that Mains was the escort commander, solely responsible for the safety of the pay, and that he, the MO, would sit where he was ordered. The actual drawing of the pay was tedious as, of course, it had to be counted and the coins checked. At this time there were no notes of a smaller denomination than five rupees, so much of the pay was in silver. Because of counterfeiting, no shopkeeper would accept a rupee coin without first banging it on a stone to see if it rang true; so one of the escort had to squat on the Treasury floor and 'ring' each rupee. A further complication came from 'deaf' coins, genuine coins which would not ring true, and additionally there were coins with Queen Victoria's head and even some of the East India Company. Although legal tender, the soldiers would not accept them, so a long altercation ensued with the Treasury officials to get them changed.

While I was at Solan, I attended my first Court Martial as 'an officer under instruction'. This meant that while I sat with and retired with the officers forming the Court and had to give my opinion as to verdict and sentence, these did not count. It was an amusing case as the culprit was the Church orderly, who was charged with obtaining cigarettes from the Canteen falsely, pretending that they were for the Chaplain. The Chaplain posted a weekly notice of the forthcoming services and the printed form had a blank space above his signature for any extra notices; foolishly he did not draw a line through this, so the orderly merely cut off the top printed part and wrote 'X packets of cigarettes' above the Padre's signature and presented this at the Canteen. The Court were extremely sympathetic towards the culprit, thinking it somewhat of a joke, and voted to give him three months detention. I, who as the most junior member had to give my opinion first, suggested six months as it was fraud by a person in a position of trust, but, of course, this had no validity. I attended three such Courts while I was with the Dorsets, but, owing to the good behaviour of the Indian and Gurkha soldier, I did not sit again for ten years, when I was the President of Summary General Court.

We arrived back in Sialkot in early October at the commencement of the glorious North Indian 'cold weather' which lasted up to early April – crisp sunny days with day temperatures of 60–70°F, but with frosts at night. The Cantonment now really woke up – field firing followed by company, battalion and brigade training, and on the social side, drink and dinner parties, polo and shooting, amateur theatricals and the Brigade Horse Show.

The Field Firing area, to which the companies went one at a time, was at Murala, the head works of the Upper Chenab Canal, about fifteen miles from Sialkot. The troops were under canvas but the officers lived in the Canal Rest House, a most beautifully kept and comfortable bungalow; I found that, during the whole of my service, the bungalows of the Canal and Forest Departments, which made money, were superior to the District Dak Bungalows and PWD Rest Houses, whose departments spent it. Evan and I got into hot water at this time – Companies marched to and from Murala so the authorities thought it a good idea for A Company returning and B Company going out to take part in an 'advance to combat' exercise. Regrettably the scheme was not properly explained and worse the umpires were late, so our respective 'scouts' duly met. No umpire described the situation to them so they merely passed each other by. Next the two vanguards met and passed each other, and finally Evan and I did the same. The umpires then arrived in furious tempers and demanded to know why on sighting each other we had not taken offensive or defensive action; we could only answer, 'No one told us to.' I remember little about collective training except that I found that the RMC had taught me nothing about the tactical handling of a platoon, so I had to hark back to what I had learnt in the OTC.

Colonel Thwaites arranged for the four of us to take a riding course at the 13/18th's manège which was great fun and at the same time I bought a horse from a Dorset officer going home; this brought me into a near collision with the Quartermaster as the horse was 'on the strength' as his charger. I must explain that, to save money, the Government of India required mounted officers to provide their own chargers – they went further and required the troopers of the part time European Auxiliary Force Cavalry Regiments to provide their own troop horses. This was not unpopular, in general, as Government paid for the upkeep of a collection of private racehorses, hunters, pigstickers and polo ponies. It was extremely popular in Indian and Gurkha Regiments who had eight mounted officers on an establishment of thirteen, so, as there were always one or two officers who did not wish to own a horse, it was not difficult to get your polo pony on the strength. It was not so popular with British Regiments, where the ratio was eight to thirty, and their agitation provoked the 'free charger' scheme in 1938. Government provided free forage and an allowance of fifteen rupees per month for the pay of the civilian *syce* (groom), but of course the mounted officer could call on his charger as required, usually in the training season. The QM sent for me and said that he would agree to keep my horse on as his charger,

The author's first polo pony, 'Joan'.

but would retain the *syce* allowance. When I protested he said I was lucky as he never used his horse – anyway if I did not like it there were many others who would agree his terms.

The horse was a 14.3 hands Meerut country bred mare called Joan; typical of her class she was very light with rather spindly legs, but was reputed to be a trained polo pony with a good turn of speed. The polo at Sialkot was of a high standard so I decided to hack her or start with a little 'stick and ball' rather than put her into a chukka. I did enter her in the Hacks and Officers' Chargers classes in the Brigade Horse Show more for fun than any hope of an award. I did discover, however, that, as she had no belly to speak of, without a 'breastplate' a government saddle was apt to finish up on her rump. My next acquisition was a brown spaniel bitch, Sally. Ownership of dogs by soldiers was strictly controlled, as a protection against rabies; it had been discovered that B Company was one over strength and Sally was that one. Sergeant Major Dutot, however, persuaded Bob Goff to allow her to be given to me as I would be leaving in a month or so; her owner was only too pleased to agree as otherwise she would have had to be put down and I was delighted to have her.

The main event of the Christmas season was the Club's production

The author with 'Sally'.

of the Ian Hay farce 'Orders are Orders' in which I had a small part. The Dorsets did not permit their officers to take leave at Christmas except for some special or family reasons, and they had to be on parade for the troops' Christmas dinners. As a result, while there was no lack of beer, there were no drink related problems and we had the troops all tucked up (often literally) by the late afternoon and the officers could then go and enjoy their dinners in the Mess. One piece of pure Kipling still persisted, the departure of a home going draft. On the march to the station came the Band, followed by the Orderly

Officer, all correctly dressed – the draft followed. The first two or three 'fours' were, in the Irish phrase, 'not drunk but drink taken'; the next lot although drunk could march, particularly if they were held up by their pals; and finally a collection of tongas, carrying those who could not even stand, brought up the rear.

The time was fast approaching when my future had to be decided. I had been interviewed by the Brigade Major, a 2nd Royal Lancer, but they had no vacancy and no other cavalry regiment had shown any interest. Colonel Thwaites was afraid that I was heading for the 'leavings' so he approached the Military Secretary, General Twiss, saying that I deserved better than that. The General, who was Colonel of the 9th Gurkhas, replied that their 2nd Battalion was under strength and had turned down two candidates on interview. He suggested that I apply and he would arrange a ten day vetting visit, promising that, if they agreed to have me, he would duly post me; he added a rider to the effect that it must be the 9th or nothing, adding as a sop, 'They play polo.' Popular Regiments – Cavalry, Gurkhas, Frontier Force and one or two others who could pick and choose their officers – operated a vetting procedure; the candidate was invited to spend his ten days' leave with the regiment. The media have on several occasions tried to misrepresent this, alleging that it was to determine the candidate's social standing, but, in fact, it was to decide if he was the type who would 'muck in', doing more than one job during the hot weather when officer numbers were down to four or five. Eventually I left for Dehra Dun, the 9th 'home' station, taking my shot gun and football boots. Actually most of the 2nd Battalion were absent on training, so I was vetted by the Depot Commander, Major Maurice Allsebrook and the subalterns of the 1st Battalion. It was a superb holiday, a shoot, a guest night in the Mess, drinks in the GOs' Club – best of all, I passed. Later on, however, I had to keep it fairly quiet that Gurkhas had not been my first choice.

I had hardly returned to Sialkot when I got an offer from Sam Browne's Cavalry but I decided that I would stick to the Gurkhas; this was a blessing in disguise, as three years later Sam Brownes were converted to a Training Regiment and the permanent officer cadre dispersed. My bearer Mohammad Ishaque did not wish to continue in my service as he was a typical British Regiment's servant, who remained with the regiment changing masters as and when the master or the regiment was ordered home. The main reason was that the IA officer, knowing the country and the language, could not be hoodwinked over the bearer's 'little bills', the money that he expended on cleaning materials, toilet paper, soap etc, which he purchased for his master and on which he got a 'rake off'. Indian Army bearers usually stayed with their masters for the whole of their service and often received a pension from them. Ishaque produced a young nephew, Mohammad Ayoub, who remained with me until 1947.

My time with the Dorsets being up and having received a posting order to the 9th Gurkhas at Dehra Dun, I obtained a horsebox from the railway and sent off Joan with her *syce*, following myself with Ayoub and Sally on 10th March 1935 and was taken on the strength of the 2/9th Gurkhas on the following day. I left the Dorsets not without some regrets – they were a first class regiment, not showy but solid worth. They treated me very well and taught me a great deal for which I shall always be grateful.

INTERLUDE

The Army in India and the Indian Army

See Appendix B – Organization of the Army in India

As existing in 1935

Many think that these terms are synonymous but they were not. The Army in India comprised all the armed forces of the Crown in India, whether they belonged to the British Army (usually referred to as the British Service) or the Indian Army. It was not subject to the control of the British War Office, but owed allegiance to the Defence Department of the Government of India. The British Service units might be described as 'on loan' to India, as India fed, clothed, equipped and paid them. This was a good bargain for the British taxpayer as he was absolved from paying for nearly half of the British Army. The personnel, officers and soldiers were subject to the (British) Army Act, but were also subject to 'Army Instructions, India' and 'Regulations for the Army in India' rather than 'Army Council Instructions' and 'Kings Regulations'. The War Office, however, retained control over appointments to command British units and the promotion of officers.

It is difficult to generalize about the composition of the Indian Army; basically it consisted of Indian soldiers, subject to the Indian Army Act, but commanded by British Officers, subject to the (British) Army Act. There were a few King's Commissioned Indian Officers, but as they were subject to the same conditions of service and held the same commissions as their British counterparts, they were usually referred to as 'British Officers'. The large influx of Indian Commissioned Officers, holding different commissions to the KCIOs, was only just starting. British Officers did not command platoons, as in the British Army, but entered as Company Officers – platoons were commanded by Indians holding commissions from the Viceroy and were junior to all British Officers.

Neither the British Service nor the Indian Army was self contained;

British units were dependent on the Indian Army for Engineer, Signal and all logistical services; the Indian Army, on the other hand, had no Field or Heavy Artillery. It had been decided, after the Great Mutiny, that Indian soldiers would no longer be trusted with artillery, which in the future would be provided by the Royal Artillery. There were, however, a number of mountain batteries on the North West Frontier manned by Sikhs and PMs, which had remained loyal; these were retained, but to maintain the fiction, they were transferred to the Royal Artillery, although the soldiers retained their Indian ranks and were subject to the Indian Army Act. This continued until 1939 when they were transferred to the newly formed Indian Artillery.

The Army's role was to repel any power attempting to invade India from Afghanistan, to contain the tribesmen on the North West Frontier, and finally to keep the peace within India. The number of British troops was 60,000 against 150,000 Indian, with a European and Anglo Indian part time force of 30,000 for internal security only. The size of the British contingent was a long standing War Office grievance; they complained that the Government of India's preoccupation with Internal Security was tying up far too many British soldiers.

The Indian Army was far more professional, as regards officers and men, than the British. While most British soldiers had enlisted only as a last resort from mass unemployment, there were far more potential Indian recruits than vacancies. The average British soldier came from the lower grades of British society, mostly from the urban poor; by contrast the Indian and Gurkha soldier came from the countryside – mainly from yeoman farmers and lesser squirearchy. There was also a strong element of son following father into the same regiment. Recruitment from the same classes and environment allowed sub units to be comprised of men from the same village or group of villages with the platoon commander, a Viceroy's Commissioned Officer, being well acquainted with the backgrounds of his men.

Loyalty to India as a country did not exist; the soldier's loyalty was to the King Emperor but to an even greater degree to the regiment – his *mam bap* (mother and father). This attitude was encouraged by the regiment which in return looked after its soldiers by the provision of amenities which the Government failed to provide – family hospitals, children's schools, provident funds and so on. The absence of 'military crime' was because the Indian and Gurkha soldier feared the indignity of a punishment far more than the punishment itself; minor derelictions of duty were dealt with unofficially by the VCOs.

There is little doubt that compulsory service in India was unpopular with the majority of the officers of the British Service – exceptions were officers of the Royal Artillery, Royal Engineers and Signals who volunteered to be seconded to Mountain Batteries, the Sappers and Miners and Indian Signals; many of these considered themselves as Indian Army and, in some cases, refused repatriation and by long Indian service augmented their pensions with an Indian service element.

General James Lunt, himself a British Service officer, writes in his book *A Hell of a Licking*:

> Although Field Marshal Montgomery would not have agreed with me, I sometimes felt that the Indian Army between the two World Wars was a more professional organization than my own. The officers were given responsibility much earlier, enjoying opportunities for active service that came rarely in the British Service until Palestine erupted in 1936. What is more, the power of the purse played little or no part in determining choice of Regiment, which was undoubtedly not the case in the British Army. Promotion was quicker too.

While it was very difficult to get rid of a young British Service officer unless his incompetence was almost beyond belief, IA officers were on probation for five years. In that time they had to obtain the Higher Standard in Urdu, pass the obligatory test in one of the regional languages spoken in their unit and finally pass the Examination for Retention in the Indian Army; should they not do so they were required to resign their commissions.

Officers of the two services met in the station Clubs, at sporting events, and at Courses of Instruction. While on the surface they were all good friends, underneath there was a certain amount of jealousy on the part of junior British Service officers – these centred around pay, home leave, promotion and responsibility. Indian Army officers received the same basic pay, but with an Indian Army allowance added; they also were credited with four first class P & O return passages. While these had to last them for the whole of their service, they could use them as they pleased, making them go further by travelling second or tourist class; this concession was not granted to British Service officers as they could be transferred to their home battalions after six years in India. IA officers received their 'second pip' at $2^1/4$ years service as against 3 for their British service counterparts, their captaincy came at 9 years and a majority at 17 – no waiting for a vacancy. I had first hand evidence of this; I attended a course at the Army Signal School as a Lieutenant with $2^3/4$ years service; also present were some of my RMC contemporaries attending as 2nd Lieutenants – they were not amused. It must have been galling for a Lieutenant of some ten years service marching at the head of his platoon to see an IA officer, sometimes only a 2nd Lieutenant, riding his horse at the head of his company.

The War Office, however, insisted that 50 per cent of all senior command and graded staff appointments in India must be given to British Service officers. This was a considerable pecuniary advantage as India paid staff officers by grade and not by rank, and at a rate considerably higher than that of the equivalent ranks. It was not unusual for a Brigade Major to be a Captain and a Staff Captain a Major. Very few Indian Army Generals, Auchinleck being an exception, ever got command of a British formation, or received staff appointments in the British Army.

Changes 1936–1939

Two major changes were:

1936 saw the start of a major influx into the Officer Corps of Indians trained at the Indian Military Academy and holding King's Commissions in HM's Indian Land Forces giving them powers of command over Indian troops only. Unlike their predecessors from Woolwich and Sandhurst, they were posted to Indianized units as platoon commanders.

The Russian/Afghan threat was downgraded in 1936 (it was revived in the 1939/40 winter as a result of Hitler's understanding with Stalin); resulting in Western Command, Baluchistan District (2nd Indian Division) with its 4th and 5th Infantry Brigades being abolished. At the same time the need for reinforcements for Burma, Malaya and the Middle East was accepted, the troops to come from Southern Command.

CHAPTER V

Dehra Dun, Birpur and the 9th Gurkhas

I DID NOT THINK that my antique car was worth taking to my new Regiment so I sold it and proceeded by train – local to Wazirabad, Frontier Mail to Lahore and after dining there, the through coach on the Calcutta Mail; this was cut off at Lakhsar Junction and attached to the Mussoorie Express coming from Delhi. I was awakened by the hubbub when the train stopped in the early morning at Hardwar, the holy city on the Ganges, where all trains halted for some twenty minutes and early morning tea could be had.

The next part of the journey was alongside the Ganges in the narrow pass where the river broke through the Siwalik Range into the plains. Once through, the line turned to the west and began a gentle climb up the Doon Valley; the first range of the Himalayas was visible to the north, and after a while the hill station of Mussoorie was sighted, the houses standing out although at an altitude of over 6,000 ft. I always found this nostalgic, as when returning from leave or from a course I felt that I was coming home. The Mess bus had been sent to meet us and, in due course, we were decanted at No 13 Bungalow from whence I walked up to the Mess for breakfast.

Dehra Dun was entirely different from Sialkot and most cantonments in Northern India, as these had been built in a rectangular shape on a flat plain. Dehra, on the other hand, was laid out on a series of plateaux intersected by rivers flowing in deep gorges and thus the roads had to conform and were seldom straight; another difference was the number of semi military and civil establishments located in the area. The climate was considerably better than that of the plains and the abundance of water made Dehra a garden city. (A detailed description is given at Appendix C.)

The 9th Gurkhas were located in Birpur, an area between the Tons and Noon rivers about two miles from the Cantonment proper. The Kitchener Reforms of 1903, besides numbering the Regiment in the

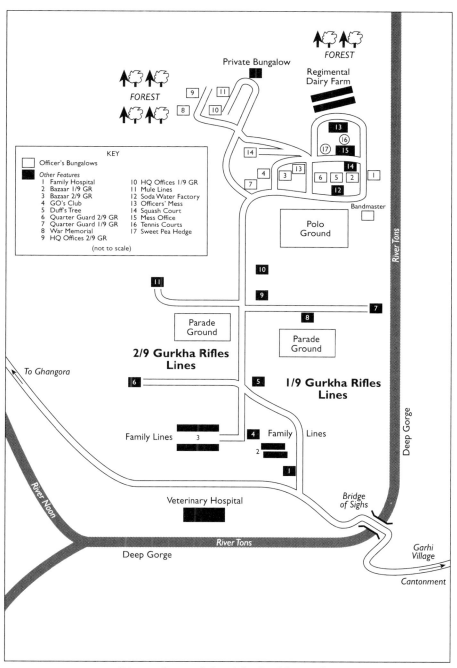

KEY

Officer's Bungalows

Other Features
1 Family Hospital
2 Bazaar 1/9 GR
3 Bazaar 2/9 GR
4 GO's Club
5 Duff's Tree
6 Quarter Guard 2/9 GR
7 Quarter Guard 1/9 GR
8 War Memorial
9 HQ Offices 2/9 GR
10 HQ Offices 1/9 GR
11 Mule Lines
12 Soda Water Factory
13 Officers' Mess
14 Squash Court
15 Mess Office
16 Tennis Courts
17 Sweet Pea Hedge

(not to scale)

Private Bungalow

FOREST

FOREST

Regimental
Dairy Farm

Bandmaster

Polo
Ground

Parade
Ground

2/9 Gurkha Rifles
Lines

To Ghangora

Parade
Ground

1/9 Gurkha Rifles
Lines

Family Lines

Family   Lines

Veterinary Hospital

River Tons

River Noon

River Tons

Deep Gorge

Deep Gorge

Bridge
of Sighs

Garhi
Village

Cantonment

Birpur: lines of the 9th Gurkha Rifles.

Gurkha Brigade, had decreed that each regiment of the Brigade should consist of two battalions. The 9th, a single battalion regiment then stationed in Landsdowne, had to move as there was no accommodation for a second battalion.

The Regiment moved to Dehra in early 1905 and, as there was no accommodation in the Cantonment already occupied by the two battalions of the 2nd Gurkhas, was sent to Birpur and encamped on the site of the future polo ground. They had two tasks: the first, which had already started, was the raising of the 2nd Battalion; this was accomplished by the simple expedient of cutting the existing regiment in half and recruiting each half up to battalion strength; the second was to build the lines, not only the troops and family accommodation but also the Mess and officers' bungalows. The planning and construction was left to the Regiment – the Government merely giving a monetary grant, which the Regimental History states was very generous.

It was decided to build the two battalion lines on a similar plan on either side of the main road – the family quarters to the south and the barracks to the north, each set of barracks being grouped around a Parade Ground; dividing the officers from the men was the polo ground, with the Bandmaster's bungalow at the end. This reflected his status – a European civilian paid by the Regiment, but wearing an officer's uniform with a Bandmaster's badges of rank.

The construction of Birpur caused great hardship for all ranks. The Regiment went into camp in the spring of 1905 and the lines were not completed until autumn 1907, entailing two summers under canvas, which the erection of grass shelters over the tents did little to alleviate. There was no piped water and all drinking water had to be brought nearly three miles from the cantonment on mule back. Electricity did not arrive until the early twenties. It was inevitable that there was much sickness and two British officers died from enteric fever. On the other hand when completed the Regiment was possessed of the best laid out lines in India.

The area chosen for the Officers' Mess and bungalows was on the site of the evacuated village of Birpur – the only building still existing in 1935 was the soda water factory, which had been used as as a temporary Mess House. Later a new mud brick building was constructed which in my day housed the Mess office and store, the library and a venue where ladies could take tea after playing tennis on the Mess courts. Eleven bungalows were constructed (No 12 was was the actual Mess); Nos 1 to 4 were three bedroomed and were for senior married officers – the remainder had two bedrooms and were designed for junior marrieds, except for Nos 5 and 6 which were used as four single quarters respectively.

Three further bungalows were built by individual officers during the Great War, and sold when the officers retired. Two were bought by the MES and numbered 13 and 14, but the third 'Bide a Wee' was sold privately to a civilian, and at this time was occupied by a Major Angelo, a retired officer of the Telegraphs Department. No 13, in which I was allotted a quarter, was built of whitewashed mud brick with a thatched roof and diamond paned windows, looking as if it belonged to the Cotswolds rather than India. It was most regrettable that in 1937, the MES rebuilt it with conventional windows and a corrugated iron roof.

By the time I joined a number of private buildings had been added to those originally constructed; the most important was the Family Hospital situated in the lower part of the 1st Battalion's family lines. The Hospital and the resident lady doctor were maintained solely at the Regiment's expense and together with the larger than life sized statue of a Gurkha soldier on the 1st Battalion's Parade Ground comprised the Regiment's War Memorial. It was discovered after delivery that the sculptor had made a serious error in transposing the haversack and waterbottle. Other additions were the Gurkha Officers' Club and the Regimental Dairy Farm – Indian and Gurkha soldiers were unable to purchase milk from the Army's military dairies, as this was reserved for officers and British soldiers, and the milk sold by the local vendors was usually contaminated. The 9th's dairy herd was of the Montgomery strain which had been developed by the Indian Agricultural Institute and was basically a cross between a Friesan bull and a local Sahiyal cow. The Regiment did its own breeding and in 1937 imported a bull direct from Holland. The Dairy buildings were near the Tons River below the Mess promontory – regrettably it did not survive World War Two as officers had neither the time nor the knowledge to run it so it was sold to the Military Farms Department.

Gurkha war memorial at Dehra Dun.

A landmark at the entrance to the lines was 'Duff's Tree' surrounded by captured Turkish guns. Sir Beauchamp Duff had been Colonel of the Regiment during the Great War.

The most striking change from Sialkot was the general appearance of Birpur and indeed the whole Cantonment – the green lawns and the profusion of flowers in the well kept gardens. The 9th Mess had sweet pea hedges ten foot high – a sight never to be forgotten. Dick Watson, who joined the 2/9th a year after me, wrote to his aunt:

> I didn't realise how foul and dusty Ferozepore was until I came here and found huge hedges of sweet peas and flowering trees with a background of hills to show it off.

Unlike the ordinary military station where units were 'birds of passage' with little interest in their environment, those in Dehra were either static, or, in the case of two Gurkha regiments, had a proprietary interest as it was their 'home station' to which they returned after a frontier tour. Bungalow gardens were kept up regimentally and the upkeep supervised and paid for by the Mess: should a bungalow be empty, the *mali* was appointed the official *chowkidar* and paid by the Government while continuing to tend the garden.

This concept stemmed from what was known as the 'Charter': an Order from the Government of India in 1864 designating 'home stations' for the then existing five Gurkha regiments and permitting them to own land and buildings. The 2nd Gurkhas owned their Mess House, Officers' Bungalows and other buildings; they also had the management of their Lines and adjacent land. The principle of the home station was later extended to the other regiments but not the concession to own land. The 9th, not being a 'chartered' regiment, would have been at the mercy of the local Military Estates Officer, who could have let the grazing around the barracks to the local cow keepers – a great nuisance. The Regiment, however, in the early days, came to an agreement to lease the whole of the Birpur area for a fixed annual rental, the area becoming known as the 'Birpur Estate'. One major advantage was that the grazing was now reserved for our own dairy cattle.

The job of Estate Officer was one traditionally given to a junior officer, so I got it. It was not considered very onerous as usually the only transaction was to receive Rs 5 from the Subedar Major for the sale of a dead tree. I got interested, however, and managed to unearth a copy of the lease and its annexed map. It so happened that in 1936 the adjacent Government Forest was due for cutting and to get the timber out, the contractor's carts would have to cross about one hundred yards of Estate land to reach a public road and we could charge him for a wayleave. He refused to pay, saying that he had every right to cross our land. My reply was to send a posse of regimental police to the scene with orders that, as soon as the carts were on Estate land to stop them, unharness the bullocks, and take them to the Cantonment 'pound' as trespassing cattle. This did the trick and regimental funds were richer by a substantial sum.

The 9th Gurkha Rifles had three peculiarities which singled it out from the other regiments of the Brigade. First, it was descended from a Bengal Native Infantry unit, which had survived the Mutiny; second, it was the only regiment to enlist the Thakur and Khas clans, the highest, after the Brahmins, in the Nepal social order; and finally, although raised later than the 1st, 2nd and 3rd Gurkhas, it was the senior regiment of the Brigade. This caused considerable resentment, but was occasioned by a decision of Government, who decreed that seniority was taken not from the date of raising but from the date of becoming a regular line regiment. The 9th entered the Bengal line as the 1/32nd Bengal Native Infantry in 1823, while the earlier three regiments did not do so until 1850 for the 1st and 1861 for the 2nd and 3rd.

There is no doubt that prior to the Great War, the Regiment was looked upon with some suspicion, if not dislike, by the other Gurkha regiments. The Thakurs and Khas, or Chettris, as they were more usually known, belonged to the Kshatriya, or warrior caste, and wore the sacred thread, while the others were Sudras or peasants who did not. While the Thakurs, as nobles, were looked up to – the King was a Thakur – the Chettris were often disliked as they provided the whole of the machinery of government from the Maharaja, the hereditary Prime Minister and Commander-in-Chief, down to the village headman and police officer. It was unfortunate that the term Chettri was also used for the offspring of a hill woman and a plains man. The other regiments were frightened that the 9th might let the side down, but their record in France, particularly at the Battle of Neuve Chapelle and in Mesopotamia, had largely dispelled this.

The Regiment was raised in 1817 as the irregular Fatehgarh Levy and renamed the Mynpoori Levy the following year. It was brought into the Line in 1823 as the 1st Battalion 32nd Bengal Native Infantry and in the following year, on the Bengal Army changing to single battalion regiments, became the 63rd BNI. Its first battle honour was earned in 1826 at the siege of 'Bhurtpore'; the second was 'Sobraon' in 1846 during the Sikh War, where a Sikh Battle Standard was captured. It was originally thought that this was the only action in which the regiment had taken part, but recent research has discovered that about one thousand Sutlej Medals inscribed Ferozeshah with clasp Sobraon had been issued to the 63rd, but for some reason they did not receive the battle honour. The Regiment became one of the first units, British or Indian, to travel by train, as they were moved in 1855 from Howrah to Raniganj on the newly opened East Indian Railway to suppress the Santhal rebellion.

The year of the Great Mutiny, 1857, saw the Regiment put to the test. Up to now, with a few exceptions, the Regiment had enlisted Brahmins, high class Rajputs and Mussulmans, mainly from Oudh and neighbouring areas and these were the classes who formed the bulk of the mutineers. The 63rd was stationed at Berhampore, where the native cavalry were showing signs of disaffection, so the authorities decided to disarm the Regiment as a precautionary measure. The Native Officers offered to hand in the weapons the day before to avoid the disgrace of a disarming parade, but this was refused. The parade went ahead and, at the conclusion, the Regiment marched quietly back to barracks from whence they performed unarmed station duties for eighteen months.

Although some men deserted, sufficient remained to warrant their rearming in 1858. This was unique as in every other case of disarming the unit disintegrated. Twelve only out of 74 line regiments remained in 1861; they were renumbered on their original seniority; the 63rd becoming the 9th, a number they have held to the present day. The original classes now accounted for only half the unit, the remainder being Bundelahs, Jats, Dogras and for the first time one company of 'Gurkhas and Hillmen'. The enlistment of Gurkhas ceased in 1881, being replaced by two companies of Nepalese Newars.

Orders were issued in 1893 for the 9th to become a class Gurkha unit, enlisting Thakurs and Khas (Chettris). These clans, although part of the original Gurkha Army of Prithvi Narain Shah, had not been enlisted for many years, not because they were bad soldiers, but because they did not get on with other Gurkhas, nor for reasons of caste would they eat with them. Colonel Vansittart, the Recruiting Officer for Gurkhas, convinced Army Headquarters that in a class unit of their own, there would be no trouble. The Regiment's title was now changed to the 9th (Gurkha Rifle) Regiment of Bengal Infantry, later to become the 9th Gurkha Rifles.

In the period up to the Great War, the Regiment saw service in the 2nd Afghan War, the 1897/8 Frontier operations and in Eastern India and was rewarded with the battle honours 'Afghanistan 1879/80' and

'Punjab Frontier'. A Maxim gun detachment was attached to the 8th Gurkhas for the Younghusband Expedition to Tibet in 1904.

The 1st Battalion was mobilized in 1914 and proceeded to France in the Meerut Division of the Indian Corps; they were in the trenches before the end of October, earning the 1914 Star with clasp (the so-called Mons Star). Before they were withdrawn to Mesopotamia in 1915, they had taken part in all major operations, earning seven Battle Honours together with the Theatre Honour 'France and Flanders 1914–15'. The Battalions changed over in Mesopotamia, the 2nd going on to gain three battle honours and the theatre honour 'Mesopotamia 1916–18'. The actions at Neuve Chapelle and Shumram Bend were selected respectively as the 1st and 2nd Battalions' 'Regimental Days'. A 3rd Battalion was raised which took part with the regular battalions in the 3rd Afghan War, the connected frontier operations gaining another battle honour 'Afghanistan 1919'.

Both battalions did frontier tours in the twenties and the 2/9th was part of the force sent to Malabar to combat the Moplah rebellion. Both battalions were part of the Emergency Garrison of Bengal sent to combat terrorism and had only just returned when I joined.

CHAPTER VI

Settling In

Birpur, Spring 1935

I SEE FROM A contemporary Army List that when I joined, the 2nd Battalion had seventeen officers 'on the book'; the establishment was fourteen, but five were seconded and three either on or about to go on long leave, so only nine were actually available for duty. This was by no means unusual at this time but it meant most officers, including the Quartermaster, taking on two or three jobs. The Indian Army did not have professional Quartermasters, the post going to any subaltern.

The Commanding Officer was 'Gag' Gouldsbury, who had been posted in only recently from the 5th Gurkhas; a first class CO, his death a year later was a great tragedy as he and his wife were very popular. The second in command, Gerry Crampton, was a rather craggy bachelor from the 1st Battalion, who had been on the staff of the Small Arms School; the only other Major, Tom Scott, a fine horseman and polo player, was the father of Lord Justice Scott of the 'Arms to Iraq' enquiry, who had been born in Birpur about the time I joined. The Adjutant was Captain George Nangle, who was to hand over in the autumn to 'Setu' White, a Subaltern who was on long leave. The other Subalterns were 'Widdy' Widdicombe, the son of a former commanding officer, 'Schultze' Keily the Quartermaster, Kenneth Boome, a University Commission, who luckily fitted into a gap above me and thus avoided going above another officer on account of his ante date, and now finally myself – a total of three Field Officers, one Captain and four Subalterns.

My first priority was to get myself properly dressed as I had now joined a rifle regiment. All my leather had to be scraped and blackened, that is my parade boots, Sam Browne belt and sword scabbard and finally my Sandhurst leggings; these although not

55

regimental pattern would be permitted until my first home leave when I could obtain those of regimental pattern from our bootmakers, Trickers. All my brass ULIA buttons and rank stars had to be replaced by black and a new rifle pattern sword hilt fitted to my sword, Mazri and silver grey shirts and green puttees in lieu of khaki had to be obtained together with a new rifle green suit of patrols; these, however, could be worn in the winter until I could obtain a new mess kit in England from our regimental tailors, Hawkes of Saville Row. Luckily I already had a pair of cavalry twill breeches with buckskin strappings, which the 9th wore in ceremonial dress instead of the more usual khaki cord.

I found that the camp kit issued in England, while excellent for a standing camp, was far too heavy for either training or frontier service so I had to purchase a number of items – a sleeping bag, a lightweight 'Hounsfield' bed and a shelter tent. Both British and Gurkha officers wore officers' pattern Mills web equipment; this also had to be obtained privately as it was not a British Army issue until 1939. There was no difficulty in putting my horse Joan 'on the strength' and as, irrespective of rank, I was going to be a mounted officer from now on – OC B Company, then Signals Officer, QM and Adjutant – she would become my charger; this required further purchases: khaki drill covers for my greatcoat and raincoat, which would be attached to the rear and front of the saddle, and my *syce*, Moti, had to be kitted out with regimental uniform – khaki shirt, breeches and puttees with black boots, together with a haversack and waterbottle.

George Nangle told me to report to Widdy, who was OC D Company but also keeping an eye on B, which was commanded by the senior Gurkha officer, Subedar Dhanraj Karki. My sojourn with D Company only lasted about two weeks during which time I met the Gurkha officers – all were Great War veterans. The Subedar Major was Shamshere Mall who was almost due for pension, the Jemadar Adjutant, Balbahadur Khattri, was selected in 1938 as one of the King's Indian Orderly Officers and Schultze Keily's right hand man was Gopi Chand, the Quartermaster Jemadar. One evening while taking Sally for a walk, the Subedar Major called me into their Club for a drink – rum. The Gurkhas used to have as 'short eats' small saucers of curried tripe, one of which was put before me. Sally had come into the Club

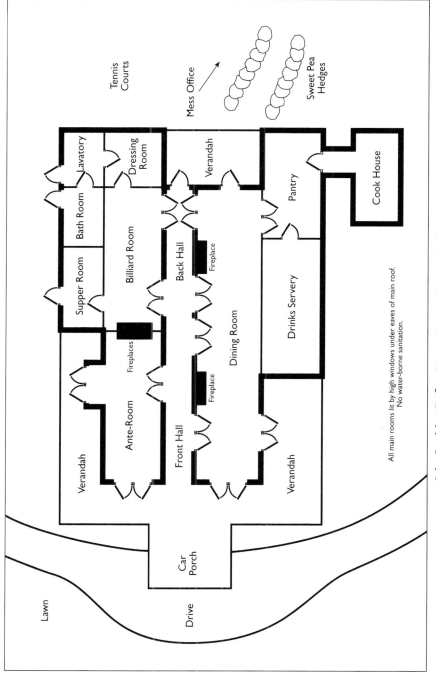

Tennis Courts

Mess Office

Sweet Pea Hedges

Lavatory

Dressing Room

Verandah

Bath Room

Billiard Room

Pantry

Cook House

Supper Room

Back Hall

Fireplace

Drinks Servery

Fireplaces

Dining Room

Fireplace

Ante-Room

Front Hall

Verandah

Verandah

All main rooms lit by high windows under eaves of main roof.
No water-borne sanitation.

Car Porch

Lawn

Drive

9th Gurkha Rifles Mess House, Birpur, Dehra Dun.

57

with me and Shamshere Mall told the orderly to put a saucer in front
of her, but before the wretched dog had had time even to sniff it,
Subedar Major Sahib fixed his eye on her and roared out '*kuttia kha*'
(bitch eat). This was too much for Sally who fled with her tail between
her legs. I had visions of being up before the Adjutant for insulting the
Subedar Major, but all was well. I duly took over B Company and my
platoon commanders were: Dhanraj himself; Nitu Khattri, who was on
leave; Bhopal Sing Bohra, one of the famous Dehra Dun family of
Bohras; and Gajendra Mall, another Dehra Dun Gurkha who had
enlisted as a Rifleman learner clerk in 1917 and finished after World
War II as a Lieutenant Colonel. He spoke perfect English and was a
great help to me in the early days. It is sad to think that so many of our
Gurkha officers perished in Malaya or in the Japanese prison camps.

The summer routine meant first parade at 6 am, or even at 5.30
when firing on the range, and went on to about 8.30. The soldiers
then had the first of their two meals; in view of the religious ritual
connected with food in peace time – ceremonial washing, removal of
boots and outer clothing – this was a lengthy affair lasting until about
10 or 10.30. Meanwhile the officers went to breakfast and were free
until 10, when they attended their respective offices – I used this time
to study for my Higher Standard Urdu and Gurkhali Obligatory
examinations. In the 2/9th officers attended office during the hot
weather in mufti, except on Friday which was the Commandant's
Orderly Room for which uniform including jackets and swords was
obligatory. The troops' morning was spent mainly in school. In the
afternoon they paraded under their Gurkha Officer Platoon
Commanders. These Parades in the 2/9th were considered GO's
Parades and, although the British Officer would often attend, he
would note how they were going but not interfere. Recreation was
followed by the men's second meal and dinner for the officers at 8.30.

The 9th Gurkhas Standing Orders stated that 'Polo was the British
Officers' game', but it was incumbent on you to play football with
your men on occasions. Unlike most Indian Army units who played
hockey, Gurkhas played football. There was no separate Polo Club,
neither did the Dehra Dun Club run the polo. It was played from
October to June on the 2nd or 9th Grounds, the Regimental Polo
Secretary being responsible for the week when play was on his

ground. Tom Scott got me playing 'slow' chukkers shortly after I joined but Joan was a disaster; she would not go near the ball, so when polo restarted in late September, I asked Tom Scott to look out for another pony. However, the problem solved itself; I tried Joan in a fast chukker and she was perfect – the poor horse was obviously bored with slow polo. I played her in tournaments from then on until we left Dehra in September 1939.

The Birpur Mess House was a revelation after the rambling hired bungalow of the Dorsets in Sialkot with furniture hired from the bazaar; by contrast the 9th Mess had been built to their design and looked as if it had strayed from a English golf club. The Hall in the centre was divided midway by an archway; in the front portion was a collection of Tibetan religious pictures brought back by the two officers who had served in the Younghusband expedition, Twiss and Collingridge. One of these pictures was sexually explicit, but unless you knew this, it looked perfectly innocuous. The rear hall had the colours of the 9th Bengal Infantry laid up on our conversion to a rifle regiment. The Ante Room and Billiard Room were on one side of the Hall and the Dining Room on the other. The Ante Room with its club fender, leather arm chairs and writing table could have been found anywhere in England. The Billiard Room displayed a Sikh Battle Flag captured at the Battle of Sobraon in 1846 and the colour staves of the 63rd BNI. The main feature of the Dining Room was the 'Rogues Gallery', the photographs of all the COs since 1890. There were a number of tiger and bearskin rugs donated by the officers who had shot them. I noticed, however, that there was no piece of silver prior to the 'Conversion Cup' of 1890; I discovered that when we were converted to Gurkhas everything possible was done to erase our 'down country' past, even to omitting the Crown which we had worn as 9 BI from our new crossed kukris badge. However, by this time it had been restored unofficially, but was only notified in Dress Regulations in 1938.

The Dorsets had run their Mess by contract, the contractor undertaking to provide the meals and kitchen staff for a fixed sum per head per day. Officers' bearers waited in Mess on a rota system supervised by the Mess Sergeant and Corporal. Indian Army units on account of the much smaller number living in generally preferred to

The Mess at Birpur.

run the Mess themselves. The 9th Gurkhas had an arrangement which fitted their service of shuttling between the home station, Dehra Dun, and frontier service. Each battalion was required to maintain a Goanese butler and cook, who besides service in Dehra Dun went to the frontier with their respective battalions. When both battalions were in Dehra, the combined force produced a butler and assistant butler, and a cook and his assistant. The small number of officers living in Mess meant that the butler or butlers were adequate for waiting at table, except on Guest nights when officer's bearers were roped in to help. A Mess *havildar* and one or two orderlies were provided from serving soldiers to have charge of the cellar and serve drinks.

Mess discipline was still very strict, although there was a great difference between a British Regiment with ten to fifteen officers living in and an Indian one with four or five. The Dorsets had insisted on the wearing of jackets and ties for breakfast and lunch, but, in the 9th Gurkhas, officers could take these meals in shirt sleeves. Dinner was a parade on five days a week, the two exceptions being Saturday and Sunday, which were supper nights. Mess kit was worn except on supper nights, when a dinner jacket sufficed. There was no such thing as a bar in the Mess – if you wanted a drink, you summoned an orderly who brought it to you in the Ante Room. On entering the Ante Room at dinner time, you said, 'Good evening, Sir,' to the senior officer present and 'Good night, Sir,' to the senior when leaving the Mess after dinner. On ordinary dinner nights you could leave the Mess as you pleased when dinner was over. Supper nights, except for the wearing of dinner jackets, were quite informal – you could eat any time between 8.30 and 9.30 and come and go as you pleased. Regimental Guest nights when all officers, included the marrieds, had to attend were held once a month and there were usually one or two Regimental Guests. This was the occasion when officers were 'dined in' or 'out' on joining or leaving the Regiment. On all Guest nights the Pipe Band played before and during dinner (the 9th had disbanded their Brass Band in 1930 on account of expense); after the Loyal Toast, four Pipers played round the table, followed by the Pipe Major alone, who on the conclusion received a large glass of rum. The Loyal Toast was drunk in the customary form on Guest nights, except that in Indian Army units the toast was 'The King Emperor'. The actual decanters were known to the Gurkha orderlies as the 'Queen'. It must have sounded odd to visitors when the President ordered the Mess Havildar to bring the 'Queen'. Unless there was some special Guest, a General or some high Civil Officer, you could leave the Mess after all Guests of your rank had gone.

Ladies were almost entirely excluded from the Mess building during this period. There was no Ladies Room in the Mess, although the 9th Gurkhas did have one in the Mess Office building, where ladies could obtain tea after playing tennis on the Regimental courts. They were invited to receptions or tea parties at the time of polo or other functions but these were always held in a marquee or on the Mess lawn and never in the Mess itself. A breakthrough occurred in 1939, when Ladies Guest Nights received official approval. It so happened that I was Vice President at the first Ladies Guest Night and when the President called 'Mr Vice, The King Emperor', I responded without thinking with 'Gentlemen, the King Emperor,' instead of 'Ladies and Gentlemen'; I was unmercifully teased as a result. The presence of ladies was anathema to some of the older officers. Maurice Allsebrook caused some amusement when, as President of the Mess Committee, he refused to have it discussed at a Mess Meeting, declaiming, 'Ordinary matters are democracy but the entry of women and dogs is discipline.'

Naturally the question of 'calling' came up but it was very different and, indeed, much simpler than in Sialkot. There were only three Messes, two Gurkha and the Royal Artillery Station Mess, but there were a number of military headquarters, organizations and quasi military establishments, not contained in one cantonment, but spread about with often as much as five miles between them. I called on the Messes, the District and Brigade Commanders and the married Officers of the 2nd Gurkhas. The 9th Gurkhas and the Mountain Gunners lived adjacent to each other in cantonments of their own, three miles from the Cantonment proper, and as our numbers were small, we all knew each other, thus calling was honoured more in the breach than in the observance. Other calling was largely a matter of individual preference – I called on the Inspector General of Forests, as he had two daughters and gave dinner parties, and also on the

Surveyor General of India and the senior Supply and Transport Officer at District Headquarters as they had daughters whom later on I used to take riding. The Deputy Commandant of the Indian Military Academy was a 9th Gurkha, so naturally I called on him. It was customary for young unmarried officers to drop in occasionally for a drink on married officers of the regiment; this was quite informal and if the host said he was busy, come tomorrow, no offence was taken.

Officers of the 9th, although members of the Dehra Dun Club, used it very little as it was in the civil lines and a long way from Birpur. We however used to patronise the weekly 'Club Night', when snacks were available at the bar, have supper, go to the cinema, which was also in the civil lines, return for beer afterwards, and then back home to bed. The Club normally ran weekly dances during the cold weather, the highlight being the New Year's Eve dance.

Another difference to Sialkot was that Saturday instead of Thursday was a holiday; this was to allow married officers to take weekend leave in the summer to visit their wives in the hill station of Mussoorie, only a forty minute drive away. There were a number of Hindu religious holidays and one of the principal, Holi, occurred shortly after I arrived. It was customary for British officers to be invited to the traditional *nautch*, actually more of a variety show than a dance, as a number of sketches were enacted, generally taking off individual British officers. An unusual feature was that the female parts in the traditional dances were taken by the younger soldiers. It was obligatory for officers to be present so leave was rarely given to British officers during Holi or the other major festivals of Dasehra and Diwali. So that I should get to know the Gurkha officers, George Nangle told me that on no account should I sit next to a British but between two Gurkha officers – somewhat of an ordeal as my Urdu was limited and my Gurkhali almost nil.

The language difficulty of newly joined officers was aggravated by Army HQ's insistence on Urdu as the official language for all regiments of the Indian Army. This may have been sound policy in the 'mixed' regiments which formed the bulk of the Army, otherwise a tower of babel would have resulted with two or three languages spoken in one unit. The emphasis, thus, was for young officers to pass their Higher Standard Urdu as soon as possible – Gurkhali was pushed into the background; the obligatory Gurkhali test was not introduced until two or three years after I joined. The actual language used in Gurkha units was Gurkhali, Urdu being spoken as a token gesture only at the time of the annual inspection.

I must emphasise the courtesy shown to me by all Gurkhas from GOs to riflemen. While my halting attempts at Gurkhali must have provoked mirth in the barrack room, it never surfaced in my presence. On one occasion when I made a mess of some orders and was apologising to Dhanraj, my senior GO, he would have none of it, putting the blame on poor Gajendra, my unofficial interpreter, saying that the Jemadar Sahib (Gajendra) must have misled me.

One of my most difficult tasks was the checking of the riflemen's sheet rolls. These allowed a man to nominate both an heir to his family pension, should he be killed or die on active service, and another heir to his estate, the balance of his pay, provident fund etc owing to him at the time of death. Many of the older soldiers left their wives in Nepal to manage the family land and took a second one to live with in the lines; all this was allowed and regulated by regimental panchayets. Thus the heir to the pension was the Nepal wife but the lines wife was heir to the estate. My difficulty was that the average Gurkha had no idea of either wife's name, and, if he had, had a great reluctance to disclose it to a stranger. However, thanks to Dhanraj and my platoon commanders, I muddled through somehow.

I have said little about the officers of the 1st Battalion as they had left for the frontier just before I arrived and only the Depot Commander, Jumbo Morris, was in Birpur. It would be two years before they returned and I would get to know them.

CHAPTER VII

Birpur – Summer and Autumn 1935

Leave and Camp

I FOUND THAT BESIDE command of B Company, I had another duty to perform, that of Accounts Officer – this was extremely tedious as in effect I was the manager and ledger clerk of the regimental private bank, the so called Treasure Chest. The Subedar Major was the cashier, who at regular intervals opened the locked box in the Guard Room to receive and pay out moneys. The battalion had public and private accounts with the Dehra branch of the Imperial Bank of India as well as as a private account with Lloyds Bank in London, and was wealthy, having private assets of about 2½ lakhs of rupees (Rs 250,000 or £15,625), compared with the 1st Battalion whose assets did not reach even one lakh.

The CO prior to Gouldsbury had been a financial wizard who had invested the battalion funds in Imperial Bank of India shares which had greatly appreciated in value. He had managed to invest some of the public funds as well. I noticed that when I made the periodical check of the cash actually in the Treasure Chest, the public funds were in debit and the private in credit; subtracting one from the other gave the amount of cash actually existing. I must confess that I found this odd, but as the practice had being going on for some time, who was I to interfere? The Controller of Military Accounts, however, woke up to this a year or so later and required the battalion to refund the public money; this was done by realizing some of the bank shares which were still at a premium – the battalion pocketing the difference.

I had passed my Lower Standard Urdu examination whilst with the Dorsets, but in the Shikasta (or Arabic) script used by most of the north Indian soldiers. Gurkhali, however, was written in the Devanagri script so I had change for my Higher Standard examination. There was a lack of official language teachers in Dehra, but I was lucky to find a young man, Taramani Pande, the son of Chintamani Pande, a retired Gurkha officer who taught in the regimental children's school. He steered me through the Higher Standard and the Gurkhali obligatory test. Taramani joined the Indian diplomatic service at Independence, becoming Consul General in New York; he retired with his English wife to St Albans, and many years later my wife and I attended his daughter's marriage to an officer of the Royal Signals.

Shortly after I joined George Nangle started to prepare the officers' leave roster for the year. Officers were entitled to two months annual leave on full pay (privilege leave) and eight months (privilege leave and furlough combined) – this when they reached the top of the long leave roster, which was every fourth year in most regiments but in the 2/9th was, at this time, every third year. Unfortunately leave had to taken in the individual training season – April to September, when the fierce heat of the 'plains' compelled officers to take their leave in a hill station or Kashmir. Another option was just beginning to become popular – two months leave out of India; by taking casual leave to get to and from Bombay, as was allowed, and travelling overland from Marseilles, five weeks less two days could be spent in the United Kingdom.

My father's health was far from good and as he was prepared to meet a part of my fare home, I put in for two months leave ex India. The officer strength had to be a minimum of only four present, but one of those on leave must be within 48 hours recall and that one was me. I told George that in that case I would not take leave that year, but the CO more or less ordered me to, saying that without it I would be fit for nothing in the autumn. I had bought a 1928 six cylinder Fiat tourer so I decided to drive up to Kashmir, diverting on the way to stay a few days with the Dorsets in Solan. 'Cag' Gouldsbury had already left on eight months leave, leaving his dog, a spaniel, in the charge of Schultze Keily. He suggested that I took the dog with me on leave as it would be company for Sally; this landed me in trouble.

While I was in Solan a Dorset subaltern and I set off on a day trek, hoping to visit an old Gurkha fort in the vicinity. Naturally we took the dogs, and after a while noticed that they were not with us so we

A typical Kashmir mountain scene.

stopped, whistled and called. Sally reappeared but not the CO's dog. We searched the area without any luck and on our return to Solan offered a reward for information but to no avail. It seemed likely that a panther had got him. Naturally I considered that this was not one of the best ways to start a career in the battalion.

My route onward to Srinagar was by the Banihal road via Sialkot and Jammu. This road, linking the summer and winter capitals of the State, had only recently been opened to public use; it had previously been reserved for the use of the Maharaja and his family. Starting from Jammu on the Punjab plain it climbed to about 6,000 ft at Batote, where I spent the night in the Dak Bungalow; it then descended to about 2,000 ft to cross the Chenab river at Ranban. After the crossing came a long climb up to the Banihal Pass, where the road tunnelled through the mountain range at 9,000 ft before descending to about 2,000 ft at the floor of the Kashmir Valley.

While gravity feed from a petrol tank under the car's bonnet was now almost obsolete, the modern pumps, mechanical or electric, were in their infancy. The usual method of transferring petrol from a tank in the rear to the carburettor was the 'auto-vac'. As this worked by creating a vacuum, its efficiency declined as the air became more and more rarefied; as we climbed the carburettor became starved of petrol, so much so that I had to make periodic stops to get petrol up to the engine – the auto-vac responding with furious clicking.

I had arranged with Evan Rowland Jones that we should take leave at the same time so that we could share a houseboat. It was quite usual to book a boat through an agency, but the actual boats were owned privately, the owner and his family living in the adjacent 'cook boat' and providing all the necessary services. The boats varied in size, but were all constructed on the same basic plan. At the stern was the lounge with a verandah, then the dining room, from where a passage ran along one side opening on to two or more bedrooms, each with its bathroom, furnished with the usual hand basin, tin bath and commode. The larger and more expensive boats often had a 'sun deck' above the lounge and were wired for electric light, as many of the moorings had electricity laid on to which the boat could be connected. There was no motive power; the boats were poled from one mooring to another. The *ghat* (mooring) rents varying according to their position.

We could only afford a small boat and a modest site at which to moor it – on the Dal Lake near the Hazratbal Mosque. My car proved to be a great blessing as we could get into Srinagar or visit the Mogul Gardens, Shalimar and Nishat, without incurring the expense of hiring a *shikara*. Quite by accident we heard of a RAMC Colonel who, with his wife and daughter, was proposing a trek along the Ladakh trail as far as the Zoji La Pass, and would be very pleased if Evan and I would join them. This was a great opportunity for us as we could not have afforded such a trek on our own. We trekked as far as the last Rest House before the Pass and then went up to the watershed and back; the Pass was snow covered but passable and we were lucky to meet and photograph two yak caravans in the centre of the Pass.

At the conclusion of my leave I returned by the same route as I had come, and all went well until just after I had crossed the Chenab at Ranban, when the car failed. Ranban had a garage who diagnosed a

Yak caravan in the Zoji La Pass.

faulty ignition coil, a minor matter if a new coil could have been obtained, which it could not. If I was not to overstay my leave, I had perforce to abandon the car and push on by such transport as I could find. It was evening, so I got a lift in a lorry to Batote where I overnighted at the Dak bungalow, proceeding the next day, again by lorry, to Sialkot. I called in at Abdullah's garage where I was known to arrange for a man to be sent up to Ranban with a coil and after fitting it to drive the car back to Dehra. Meanwhile I hoped to get a seat in the daily Srinagar–Lahore touring car service, which should pass through Sialkot about 5 pm. Something, however, had gone wrong and when by 7 pm the car had not turned up I took a seat in a lorry, arriving at Faletti's Hotel at Lahore about midnight. The next day I took the train to Dehra. I reckoned that instead of an expenditure of ten rupees to obtain and fit a coil, had one been available at Ranban, the breakdown had cost me nearer two hundred, which as a subaltern I could ill afford. One facet stood out: the trust in the integrity of the British officer; Mr Abdullah was prepared to trust me to pay him after the car had been delivered, and Faletti's accepted my cheque without any hesitation.

The hot weather and monsoon routine was not particularly exciting, but this one was enlivened by the annual inspection and the saga of the eight surplus rifles. The inspection was officially carried out by the District Commander, General Jack Collins, but really by the staff officers that he brought with him; they would poke their noses into anything that they thought fit. It was possible that one such might count the arms in one of the rifle kotes to see that the total tallied with the kote register. The Battalion had returned from Mesopotamia in 1919 with two Bar and Stroud rangefinders, two Vickers machine guns, eight service rifles and a quantity of 303 ammunition, surplus – how or why these items had been acquired had long since been forgotten, but I suspect that they had been retained 'in case they might come in useful'. The rangefinders and the MGs were no problem, they had been broken up for unauthorized repairs and the ammunition had been buried, but the rifles remained.

Gerry Crampton was acting CO, supported by some three or four subalterns, including the QM, Schultze Keily. Gerry was a very great gentleman and one to whom the telling of a lie was anathema, so Schultze locked up the rifles in an empty GO's married quarter, but thought it wiser not to tell him. As luck would have it, when the official cortège was near the GO's quarters, the General, who was British Service, expressed a wish to see one, and Gerry, pointing to the one which housed the rifles, ordered the keys to be brought. After some time, it was explained that the keys could not be found, so another quarter was opened. Everybody except Gerry knew the reason and later a full confession had to be made. Most COs would have been very angry and handed out reprimands all round but not Gerry, gentleman that he was – all he said was, 'You know, old boy, they might have told me.'

Over the years, as my experience increased, especially as for long periods I was Quartermaster or officiating Adjutant, I got the hang of these inspections; it was not difficult, if you were an efficient unit, to get good marks from the inspecting Generals. The Army Commander, 'Dolly' Baird, not a General who inspired great confidence, was apt to add the odd derogatory remark to show that he was on the ball such as 'the head ropes of the officers' chargers were badly tied' or 'the officers' chargers looked a weedy lot' – I was not surprised as they had been playing polo for the previous six months. Dolly Baird was an Indian cavalryman whom Haig had taken home in 1912 and who was on his staff during the War, and who subsequently had been on someone's staff all his career. It was the state of the unit's arms and equipment which mattered and the inspectors were the Brigade Ordnance Warrant Officer (BOWO) and the Chief Civilian Master Armourer (CCMA). The former had the most excellent relations with our highly efficient senior 'Q' clerk, Havildar Saligram Sahi, who amended and kept up to date his, the BOWO's, various manuals and instructions. The CCMA carried out his inspection of arms separately – an operation taking several days. It was imperative that the QMJ attended to ensure a constant flow of bottles of beer. All this paid handsomely and we received an 'excellent report' for three or four years running.

The monsoon ended in early October and Dehra Dun dried up. I had to apply my mind now to commanding my company during field firing, platoon and company training. I had to oversee my platoon commanders' training of their platoons and later to set my own schemes for company training. I remained in command of the company during battalion and brigade training; in fact, during this period I was the only British company commander, the other companies being commanded by GOs. I was lucky to have Gajendra in my company as Battalion orders were given in Gurkhali and I used to take him to the CO's order group to help me out if I got stuck. I now realized the difference in status of a 2nd Lieutenant in the Indian Army. This was brought home to me when in camp for field firing. I found that a sentry had been posted over my tent and the first time I came out in the morning he presented arms and the guard turned out. I then realized that as a detachment commander I was entitled to the compliments paid to a Field Officer. The same occurred in barracks as BOs, irrespective of rank, took turns as Field Officer of the Week, instead of Orderly Officer.

Brigade Training based on a Field Army role was to be undertaken from a camp near Roorkee as there were few facilities in the Doon Valley for such training. Our CO decided that company and battalion training would be carried out from a standing camp adjacent to the site of the future Brigade camp, and as we were likely to be in camp for nearly two months, tentage on a lavish scale was hired – each officer would have a 'Tent Staff Sergeant', a large square tent, with a small ridge tent adjacent as a bathroom, and furnished with the camp bed, table, and chair that I had been issued with in England. Two large marquees were erected for the mess ante and dining rooms each with a mud brick fireplace for the cold evenings; small tents were adjacent as pantry and servery. Further tentage was provided for the cook house and individual and mess servants.

While the soldiers' baggage was lifted in government transport, officers' servants, excess baggage, mess servants and stores were taken in the private mess bus. This vehicle, a Morris Oxford with a special body, could seat six, exclusive of the driver, together with a large space at the back for baggage. It could be hired by officers as required and was much in demand at weekends by officers wishing to go into Dehra, some thirty miles away. Those of us who had cars took the first opportunity to collect them and bring them to camp; our horses had accompanied us on the march out.

The only married officer affected, Tom Scott, could still get home most weekends; although I was missing the polo, I very much enjoyed this my first battalion camp – the glorious fresh sunny weather, not too hot, and the cold nights when we would gather for pre dinner drinks before the ante room fire. We were close to both the Ganges and Jumna Doabas, which abounded in snipe as well as the occasional duck, so we were out shooting most weekends – all told we had some four or five cars available, so transport was no problem. I think most of all I enjoyed the comradeship, both with my brother officers and with those incomparable gentlemen, my Gurkha platoon commanders.

We arrived back from camp in mid December when plans were being made for Christmas. I regret to say that although it was a statutory holiday, the religious aspect was largely ignored by single British officers; indeed many of them considered their men's festivals more important. Shortly before we went into camp, the Battalion celebrated the Gurkhas' main festival, Dasehra, dedicated to the goddess Kali. This was a ten day holiday during which on 'Kali Ratri' a young buffalo is decapitated at midnight with one stroke of a ceremonial kukri. On the following morning a large number of goats are sacrificed, but to good purpose as the battalion had been drawing and hoarding its meat ration 'on the hoof', so the the dead goats were used for a feast that evening. At the same ceremony the regimental Pandit blessed a selection of the unit's arms. British Officers were expected to attend, and at the second ceremony, a new officer was invited to sacrifice a goat; while he could refuse, this act gave great pleasure to the Gurkha Officers and other ranks. I duly did my part. To assist you, you were allowed to use two hands and the goat was held.

Most of the single officers went off to a three or four day shooting camp and Schultze asked me to accompany him to a place called Tip in Bijnor District, where the Regiment had been shooting since coming to Dehra. I remember little of this camp, except that on the second evening, a police constable appeared ordering us off, on the authority of the District Superintendent of Police who was camping nearby. We refused to obey and sent back a note saying that our regiment had shot at Tip for many years. The next morning came a note saying, 'If you won't go, you had better join me,' together with an elephant and a bullock cart to move our gear. We had two or three very enjoyable days with the SP, one Marsh Smith, a senior UP policeman, before returning to Dehra in time for the New Year's Eve dance and the Proclamation Parade on New Year's Day.

CHAPTER VIII

1936 – Leave to England

Promotion and Army Signal School

THE YEAR 1936 saw a considerable rationalization of the Indian Army's Officer Corps as a result of the introduction of the Special Unemployed List and the 'Hungry Hundred' Schemes. The SUL was a form of voluntary or compulsory redundancy affecting Majors and senior Captains, designed to break the promotion block – a hangover from the Great War. Those selected would retire on a special pension but would be liable for recall in the event of a national emergency. Allsebrook, who was on long leave, and de Wilton, who was with the Assam Rifles, were selected. There was no doubt about the latter, but Allsebrook, who was a very popular officer, was brought back at the conclusion of his leave and kept hanging about doing extra regimental jobs while his case was being decided. He finally tired of the uncertainty and applied for voluntary inclusion. Both officers were recalled in 1939 and Allsebrook commanded the Battalion in Malaya with great gallantry before becoming a POW of the Japanese.

To overcome the chronic shortage of junior Captains, one hundred British Service Lieutenants (the Hungry Hundred), of over nine years service were invited to transfer with immediate promotion to Captain. The 2/9th got two, both from the Hampshire Regiment (Robinson and Hudson) and 1/9th one (George), from the Somerset Light Infantry. While they differed considerably in temperament, all three were an asset to the regiment – two commanded battalions in World War II and the other, who was a prisoner of the Japanese, was the last British Commandant of the Regimental Centre.

'AO' Robinson was a very professional officer, who had been an instructor at Sandhurst, but he was very highly strung and apt to get into a flap; he did not do much regimental service as he went off to the Staff College and then only returned for short periods between

74

staff appointments; he was on the staff of III Indian Corps in Malaya before becoming a prisoner of the Japanese. He was later the last British Commandant of the Regimental Centre. John Hudson was the complete opposite, completely unflappable and never doing a job of work if he could get someone else to do it. His father was a senior member of the ICS, while he himself had been ADC to the GOC Peshawar District, 'Daddy' Coleridge. He was a typical regimental officer, staying with the battalion until he was ordered to Norway in spring 1940, from whence he returned with a well earned MC. He finally commanded the 1st Battalion, with great distinction in Italy and Greece.

At the same time we acquired a new 2/Lieutenant from the ULIA, Dick Watson — very tall, with a craggy face, he was given the nickname 'Strangler'. He had come to Sandhurst from the ranks and was in every way a first class officer and a good comrade. His death in 1939 as a result of a tussle with a tiger left a gap in the officer structure very difficult to fill. Strangler came to B Company to understudy me and on my proceeding on short leave home took over command; he remained with the company during 1936 and 1937.

At this time Cag Gouldsbury died after a short illness, a great tragedy as he was much liked and respected. A problem arose over his funeral. He was a lapsed Catholic and, at the time of his death, could be said to have no religion. The Anglican chaplain said it was none of his business to bury him and his Catholic colleague, at first, took the same line. This created a serious problem — the absence of a proper military funeral would not be understood by the Gurkha officers, who naturally would wish to pay their last respects. After some persuasion, however, the Catholic padre relented to the degree that while he still refused a funeral Mass in his Church, he would attend and conduct a short service at the interment. His death caused a serious imbalance in relative seniority of the regiment's senior officers, but this was of little concern to me and anyway I was about to proceed on leave home.

I had been granted two months leave ex India from middle March, not an ideal time as I would return in the middle of the hot weather, but as the most junior officer I had to accept what I was offered. It so happened that Ken Boome was proceeding on long leave at the same time, so we decided to travel together. I could only afford second class and Ken also wished to eke out his government passages by doing the same. I must add that in order to clear cabins for the popular Riviera–England sea voyage, the P&O would provide rail tickets of the equivalent class, Marseilles–London or vice versa. We found that the P&O were running an extra boat leaving Bombay on 14th March. This was the *Moldavia* of 16,000 tons which had been demoted from a I and II class mail run to a one class II class voyage to and from Australia with fares equated to the type and position of the cabin. We found that we could get berths in a three berth cabin at a cheaper fare than that charged on a mail boat.

The *Moldavia* had retained her two dining saloons, the old I class forward and the II class aft, each with two sittings – our cabin's position gave us seats for the first sitting in the forward saloon. Neither of us relished dining at 6.30, so we approached the head waiter who reallocated us to the second sitting aft. We found at our table two conductors, and their wives, of the Indian Army Corps of Clerks, with whom we had little in common. After dinner Ken looked at me and said, 'A little expenditure of money, I think, is necessary' – so back we went to the head waiter, rubbing our noses with £1 notes. The result – places at the doctor's table, the other occupants being four of the most gorgeous Australian girls. This ensured a very pleasant voyage.

My return trip was on the *Viceroy of India* – at that time one of the newer P&O ships and the last to be painted in the traditional colours of black hull and funnel and brown upperworks. She was also one of the first all electric ships, her steam turbines' only function being to generate electricity for all purposes, propulsion, winches etc as well as for domestic use. My father had very kindly paid for a berth in a double cabin on the P&O Express, Calais to Marseille, avoiding all the hassle of changing trains in Paris.

It was a memorable journey. It so happened that the King of Egypt had died suddenly and his heir, Farouk, was a Cadet at Woolwich. The British Government laid on a destroyer to take him to Calais, where he joined the P&O Express, and persuaded the P&O Company to divert the *Viceroy* to Alexandria to disembark him. This meant a most diverting trip for the other passengers – a Guard of Honour with Band of the Garde Republicaine at the Gare de Lyon, all the top brass coming out in their launches to pay their respects at Malta and complete chaos at Alexandria where the launches of the Royal Navy, the Egyptian Navy and every conceivable organization jostled for position at the *Viceroy*'s gangway. A bonus for us passengers was that to make up time to fulfil the mail contract the passage of the Red Sea was faster than usual. As it was out of season the ship was almost empty – only about twelve passengers in I Class and about double this number in II. I had a large four berth cabin to myself.

I found on my return that I was to turn over B Company to Strangler Watson. The Signals Officer, Malcolm McGill, had departed to the Burma Frontier Force, and I was to take his place, which involved also the command of HQ Company, and, at the same time, I had to prepare myself for the Course at the Army Signal School. This was quite an ordeal as every entrant was required to achieve the standard of a trained signaller, involving sending and receiving in the Morse code in Flag, Heliograph, Lamp and Buzzer, and any failure to 'pass in' meant a return to unit with a black mark against both the officer and his unit. Luckily one of the Signal Naiks, Bhim Sing Bohra, the younger brother of my platoon commander in B Company, could speak some English – he became my instructor and rigged a line between my bungalow and the Signal Platoon's barrack, on which every evening we practised sending and receiving in Morse.

The summer continued on its dreary way, but at least for a few weeks, until the onset of the monsoon, there was polo and later I tried my hand at fishing. Setu White was a keen fisherman and used to take me out on Sundays to fish one or other of the Doon rivers for mahseer. I never caught anything but it was a pleasant relaxation. I would add that several writers have said that mahseer tasted like cotton wool full of pins.

I joined the Army Signal School at Poona at the end of September – the Course's duration was of one or two days short of three months; this was a cunning move by Military Finance to avoid having to pay permanent move allowances; a permanent move was for three months or over. September was still part of the Poona 'season' – the Governor was still in residence and the race meetings were continuing. Another amenity was the 'Deccan Queen', the fastest train in India. An electric corridor train with a restaurant car, it left Poona at 7.45 am and arrived at Bombay at 11.00; it returned at 5.45 pm arriving at Poona at 9 pm – breakfast going down and dinner coming up. Naturally this facility was much used by officer students taking day leave to Bombay on the Thursday holiday.

I did not enjoy the Course – I must say straight away that I was not 'course material'. I found the instruction by British NCOs very tedious and hidebound; everything was done 'by the book' and little deviation was allowed. Towards the end we did field exercises on how to organize a battalion's communications during various types of training. I thought at the time how useless this was, as in actual fact, I would have to arrange our communications as my CO wanted it and not how the School taught it. More than that, I missed my riding and particularly my polo. My position was made worse as there three or four 2nd Lieutenants from British Regiments who had been my contemporaries at Sandhurst; the fact that I was a Lieutenant (promoted 2nd May) did not please them. Nevertheless I finished the course with a reasonably good report.

Two memorable events occurred whilst I was on the course. The first was the abdication of King Edward VIII; it so happened that when the news came through I was on a joint exercise with the Indian Wing. The reaction of the Indian NCOs in my syndicate was: 'If the Padishah wanted a "nautch girl", why should he not have one?' and anyway 'it was all the fault of the Padre Sahibs'; the second event was the death of my father.

I knew that his Executors and Trustees were my aunt, my father's sister, and a widowed lady whom he might have married had he been in better health. I had reason to believe, also, that the estate was considerable but matters were complicated as the bulk of my father's estate was derived from my grandfather who had died less than two years before, with the resultant double death duties. It behoved me therefore to go home as soon as I reasonably could. I was due for long leave in 1937 and as I was in Poona, the easiest course would have been to take my leave direct from there.

The Battalion were prepared to grant my leave but pointed out that as I had not passed my Retention Examination, I would be unable to use one of my free return passages. They suggested that I returned for Christmas, passed the examination, and then proceeded on leave. In the meantime, I booked a I class passage with Cook's, Bombay, on the *SS Comorin* sailing on 5th January 1937. I paid for this myself, increasing my overdraft with Cook's (Bankers) on the understanding that they would receive the refund direct from Government. However after I had arrived home, the Battalion informed me that the CMA had refused the refund on the grounds that I had not obtained their Form 'X' before booking the passage. It was pointed out to them that I was not entitled to the Form as I had not passed the Retention Examination. They replied that I could have obtained the Form, but must not use it until I was qualified, and anyway they could not override statutory rules – only the Secretary of State or the Governor General in Council could do that. They suggested that as I was in England, I should apply to the India Office. It so happened that one of my godfathers was a high official there so the matter was quickly resolved.

CHAPTER IX

1937 – Long Leave to England and a New Commanding Officer

I DULY PASSED MY Retention Examination and set sail for England on the RMS *Comorin* on 5th January. I had a single berth cabin on the boat deck; this was in a deckhouse of five or six such cabins, with adjacent bathroom and lavatories reserved for male passengers. In contrast to the amenities on cruise liners today, the accommodation provided, except on the Atlantic run, was, even in I class, spartan. Most of the principal lines relied on mail contracts, so passengers came second. I have recounted in the previous chapter how the Viceroy of India's voyage in May could hardly have been viable in terms of passenger revenue but, passengers or no, a P&O liner sailed each week to fulfil the mail contract.

Before the universal use of air mail, the sea mail arrangements were very elaborate and speedy. The Indian mails closed in London in the evening of Thursday and went by special train to Dover, crossing the Channel by special boat. Another special train for Marseilles awaited them; they travelled in the charge of two British postal officials, arriving at noon on Friday, and were then loaded on to the Bombay steamer under the watchful eye of the ship's Mail Officer, by tradition the 2nd Officer. As there were a number of bags of registered and insured mail, a good deal of checking was necessary. When all the outward mail had been unloaded, the train was shunted to the berth of the incoming steamer to pick up the English mail and, in the charge of the same British postal officials, returned to Britain, reaching London on Saturday. In the opposite direction, the Bombay mail boat left at midnight on the Friday and, after calling at Malta, Port Said and Aden, reached Bombay in the afternoon of Thursday, thirteen days later. Awaiting the boat at Ballard Pier Station were the Imperial Indian Mail for Calcutta and the Frontier Mail for Peshawar. These trains with their postal sorting vans took care of mails for north, central, east and north east India. Mails for the south were dispatched by the ordinary mail trains.

Until the arrival of the 'Strath' class, the first the *Strathnaver* of 21,000 tons in 1931, there were near enough no cabins with facilities, only wash basins, and few if any double cabins with two side by side beds, upper and lower berths being the norm. I was lucky to obtain a single cabin as these were in very short supply, double and often three berth cabins being usual even in first class. Passengers could not take a bath when they wished as this was linked to dressing for dinner which was *de rigeur*; besides the cabin steward, there was the bath steward who arranged bath times. At the allotted time he would escort the passenger to the bathroom, where he had prepared a bath of hot sea water, with a small tub of fresh water on a board across the tub.

Public rooms and deck space were spacious, certainly in first class, but except for the *Viceroy* which had a proper swimming bath in the bowels of the ship, and the new *Straths* which had them on deck, the older ships had only a makeshift plunge bath on the forward well deck. The meals in the P&O were gargantuan, five and six courses at lunch and dinner, including the inevitable curry. The smoking room bar closed at about 10.30 pm but hungry and thirsty passengers could obtain at any hour of the night beer and sandwiches in the dining saloon from the night watchman.

The *Comorin*, and the 'C' class in general, were too small to merit a 'Staff Captain' as second in command and charged with administration, so this and, in particular, passengers' amenities were carried out by the Chief Officer and as I was young and single he asked me to assist him. I cannot remember exactly what I did, except that I won the table tennis tournament and still have my prize, an ashtray. Two Gurkha subalterns were on board, James Showers of the 1st and Wilfred Oldham of the 4th; both were ekeing out their government passages by travelling second. As I was precluded from entertaining them in the I class public rooms, the Purser very kindly arranged for whisky and short eats (caviar) to be served in my cabin.

I finally arrived at Victoria Station on a cold January evening and took a taxi to the Chiswick house to stay with my aunt. I was soon involved in assisting the Trustees in sorting out my father's estate. My grandfather had refused a suggestion that he should leave his possessions in trust for me with a life interest to my father and my aunt which would have saved one set of death duties – these were very heavy in my case, as the two male members had died within eighteen months of each other. Instead he left the Chiswick house to my aunt, but the contents and his investments jointly to my father and aunt. My father had left all that he was possessed of to me in trust, with the proviso that I received the income, but not the capital until I was thirty or married with the approval of the Trustees. The actual position when I came home was that my father had received the half share of my grandfather's investments, but not his share of the house contents as he was living there. The winding up my father's estate was going to be a considerable burden to two elderly ladies, the Trustees.

My aunt and I agreed that, for the time being, the house's contents should remain in situ as I had no use for them and anyway the Chiswick house would continue to be my English home for the time being. My aunt later moved all the contents to a Putney maisonette, when the Chiswick house had to be evacuated owing to bomb blast and they remained intact until I came home married in 1953; even then no division was made as my wife and I only took such pieces as we needed for our new home. To ease the Trustees' burden my father's old Clerk in Chambers agreed to oversee the Trust without any fee – an act for which I shall always be grateful. My father's estate was sworn at about £20,000, which after payment of death duties would produce before tax about £900 a year over and above my pay. I was going to be a very wealthy subaltern indeed and further, on the death of my other grandfather I would be possessed of another very substantial sum; looking back I wonder if a private income was good for me as I was able to do and take such jobs as I wished rather than those which would further my career.

One of the first things I had to do was to organize transport, I had not got a UK driving licence; in the previous year I had driven on an International Permit issued in India by virtue of my Indian Licence, but coming home this year in a hurry, I had neglected to get one. I consulted the AA, who made an appointment for me to be tested by an examiner whom they had on the premises of their Head Office in Coventry Street, and additionally they would provide a car for the test – driving from Coventry Street to Trafalgar Square and back; the traffic was very different then. I passed, my provisional licence was duly endorsed and I was now licensed to drive. My father had bought for me the year before a second hand Morris saloon which I found both too small and too slow and quite unsuited to Indian roads should I wish to take it back with me, so I traded it in for a Ford V8. This was a 22 hp model; the original V8s were 30 hp, but as, at that time, British car tax was linked to horse power, Fords decided to market a model which would attract less tax. I did not know it at the time, but my purchase was an experimental model with the 30 hp chassis and body but with the new 22 hp engine on a special mounting. It was an excellent car except for the headlights which were dim, probably because of the 6 volt battery. I found a firm which specialized in headlights and had mine changed without having to change the battery.

Compared with most subalterns of my age I had a very quiet leave; I had no relatives, except for my aunt on my father's side and besides my grandparents only two aunts and two cousins on the other. My cousins were younger than I, one still at school. The lack of brothers and sisters meant that I had few friends of my own age. One of the Australian girls from the *Moldavia* was living in London and I saw something of her; she was a keen rider so we hired horses on Sundays from the famous stable off Sloane Street to ride in Rotten Row. This involved crossing Knightsbridge at the traffic lights by the French Embassy. Traffic lights in those days were controlled by a pressure pad, so if they were at red the horse had to dance on the pad to get them to change.

Another diversion during my leave was to attend a Sovereign's 'Levée', the male equivalent of the 'Debs' presentation, which was still in existence, and officers were supposed to attend, on first commission, on attaining field rank and every step after that – for practical reasons first commission for IA officers was interpreted as first long leave. Service Dress could be worn and King George V had stated that he preferred to see officers in well tailored Service Dress than in ill fitting Full Dress, obviously borrowed from Regimental Tailors. Few Regiments, however, would have permitted their officers to wear anything but Full Dress. I was therefore fitted out by Hawkes, including a white Wolsely helmet with a black spike and silver regimental badge. I was summoned to attend the first Levée of King George VI. The procedure was: being lined up in the Throne Room between two Court officials; on their command 'Go', marching forward, while someone announced, 'To be presented, Lieutenant Antony Mains'; turn left to face the King, bow, turn right and march out – not even a glass of sherry. The only advantage was that no application for entrance to the Royal Enclosure at Ascot would be entertained without having been presented.

I did two trips abroad. In the spring I took my aunt to Vienna and Innsbruck, as a sort of thank you for all that she had done for me. In the late summer, my elder cousin and I went on a car trip to the Belgian Ardennes and Luxembourg. Motoring abroad was very different then. In the first place there were no car ferries; cars were taken, crane loaded, on the ordinary passenger ships. The documentation was considerable as each European State charged duty on used cars as well as on new ones, so the AA or RAC had to guarantee the duty in case the car was not re-exported. The usual document issued by the motoring organizations was the 'Carnet de Passage au Douane': a massive tome with a separate page for each frontier to be crossed. The page was in three parts, two tear off portions and a counterfoil. On entry the customs filled up and retained the IN portion and stamped the counterfoil. On leaving the OUT portion was dealt with. The Carnet had to be returned, in my case, to the AA as proof that the car had not been left behind in a foreign country.

One of the girls that I met up with was somewhat older than I and interested in good works. She persuaded me to help out on a charity cruise on the Thames; the ship had a special licence, which allowed drink to be sold on board at any time. A number from stage and screen came and one, the actor Ralph Lynn, got very merry. At the conclusion I went ashore at Chelsea Pier at 3 am with my girl friend, clutching a canvas bag of the takings, about £300, a very large sum in those days, and hoping that a taxi would shortly appear.

I was lucky that Chiswick was close to Richmond Park; I had started to ride again during the RMC vacations at the Equestrian Club at Ham. The Club was owned by a Captain Tom Brigg, a war time Indian Cavalry Officer; his father was the head of the firm of

Brigg's umbrellas, later to merge into the West End firm of Swayne, Addeney and Brigg. Tom Brigg was a member of a well known polo team 'The Trailers'; the other members were the Anglo-Argentine Johnny Trail and his two sons. Johnny kept his ponies at the Equestrian Club during the season, and it was suggested that after they had arrived from the Argentine, I should come over early on most mornings to help school and stick and ball them. When the season started, I played three days a week on the old Ham ground, now built over; I hired a couple of ponies from Tom Brigg which gave me four chukkers. It occurred to me that it would be a good idea to buy a pony in England, play it to the end of the season and then ship it out to India; this I could well afford to do.

While playing at Ham I had one of the worst crashes of my polo career; the Prince of Berar, the son of the Nizam of Hyderabad, endeavouring to ride me off almost at a right angle, mistook his direction and crashed at full gallop into the hind quarters of my pony. The pony and I went down, the girth broke and I was left on the ground with the saddle as the pony got up and galloped away. I was not seriously hurt, only very bruised and battered. It was unfortunate that I had arranged to go after polo with Billy Walsh, Tom Brigg's head groom, to look at a pony for sale north of London; driving was agony. I seem to have been unlucky with saddles coming off − the following year, my CO, Bertie Nepean, lent me a pony for a tournament in Dehra Dun, but insisted that I used his tack − the saddle came off when I was going flat out, but luckily I was little damaged. Much later when I was at the Staff College and was teaching Pauline, my second wife, to ride, the girth on a horse that I had borrowed for her broke and she came off and suffered mild concussion.

I eventually bought a very nice 15 hands pony named 'Grave Lady' and played her for the rest of the season, after which her shoes were taken off and she was put on low energy feeds prior to shipment. As far as I remember, I paid fifty guineas for her and another fifty pounds for shipment; adding in the cost of a horsebox from Bombay, she probably cost me between fourteen and fifteen hundred rupees. I expected that after playing her for one or two seasons I could have sold her for at least two thousand − alas, the War put paid to that.

During the last fortnight of my leave I met and fell in love with Beryl Kavanagh, who lived nearby and whom I had known as a teenager. She had just returned from a two year stay in India with her uncle, a Major Phelps of the Dogras. We agreed that we would leave matters in abeyance, but, if possible, I would come home on short leave in 1938, and if our feelings had not changed, we would announce our engagement.

About ten days before my departure for Marseilles, I drove the V8 to Tilbury for shipment on the steamer on which I would be travelling – another 'C' Class P & O. As far as I remember the charge was the same as for Grave Lady, about £50. The car was collected at Bombay by the Ford organization and taken to their Depot at Colaba for a check up before I set off to drive it to Dehra; this abutted on to the drying grounds where the famous 'Bombay Duck' was prepared. The stench of rotting fish had to be smelt to be believed.

There was not much long distance motoring in India in the thirties and the roads outside the Punjab and NWFP were primitive. The Bombay–Agra Road, second only to the Grand Trunk Road in importance, had long untarred stretches and where it was tarred, this was only a narrow strip in the centre of the carriageway. Maintenance was in the hands of some five different Public Works Departments – the extremities were the responsibility of the Bombay and UP PWDs and the centre portion of Indore and Gwalior States together with the Government of India's PWD for those sections where the princely States were too small or backward to look after a road of that importance. There was little traffic and where the road surface was good forty five to fifty miles could be done in the hour. I made the Dak Bungalow on the banks of the Nerbudda River on the second night and my luck was in as the bridge was open, although this was September in the monsoon season. The bridge was a curiosity; it was built with about twenty very narrow and solid arches and no parapets, only a flimsy metal handrail which was removed during the monsoon. Although the road was about twenty feet above the river, when in spate the river flowed over it. The current was too strong for a ferry so traffic had to wait patiently until it subsided.

The fourth night was spent at the new Hotel at Gwalior which the Maharaja had built in conjunction with Imperial Airways as a lake in the vicinity was a staging post on the England–Australia Flying Boat service. The road between Gwalior and Agra crossed the river Chambal by a bridge of boats, which was replaced during the monsoon by a manual ferry which could only take one lorry or two cars at a time. My luck was in: the ferry was on my side of the river and my car was the only one waiting to cross. From then on it was plain sailing, except that I had problems with the electric petrol pump, which worked erratically in very high temperatures; this was endemic in most new models and was later corrected by placing an asbestos shield between the pump and the engine. I found that in very hot weather, on no account should the engine be switched off immediately after coming to a stand, but it should be allowed to idle so that the carburettor could fill up.

With the Signals Course and Long Leave, I had, in fact, been absent from the Battalion for nearly a year and considerable changes had taken place; I had hardly met the new CO, who had joined us only a short time before I went to Poona. He was another 5th Gurkha, Bertie Nepean, and was as typical of his Regiment as 'Cag' Gouldsbury was not. The 5th maintained that they were the most efficient and their men the most courageous in the Gurkha Brigade, and did their utmost to prevent their officers leaving for the Staff or outside employment. Nepean had been connected with the famous 5th Gurkha, Villiers Stuart, who had an irrational dislike of all Gurkhas other than Magars and Gurungs. Line Boys were anathema to him and he equally disliked Nepal born Chettris. He once wrote of them 'whom our men disliked and on no account would we enlist them.' Nepean soon showed his dislike of our somewhat easygoing ways, which were very different from the rigid officer's discipline of the 5th. However after a while he mellowed, when he discovered that we were just as efficient as the unit from which he had come.

He remained intransigent in his dislike of the Chettri clans and more so of educated Gurkhas – poor Gajendra soon fell foul of him and Bertie intended to block his promotion to Subedar and discharge him as a Jemadar. He was saved by Tom Scott's vehement opposition, but Bertie showed his spite by making him Education and Intelligence Officer – an appointment normally held by a Jemadar. There was no doubt that Bertie was unpopular with the other ranks – Gajendra

B Company football and tug of war teams, 1936.

wrote in his Memoirs that he was nicknamed in Gurkhali 'the leopard' as he was always ready to pounce on any irregularity and to find fault whether there was any or not.

Tom Scott and John Hudson were the permanent members of our more senior cadre – a number of others came and went for short periods between staff jobs, but except for Nick Hurst who was with us for some time as Recruit Company Commander and for a while was Second in Command while Tom Scott was on leave, they made little impact. Nick had an impressive war record, MC and Bar, and was popular with those of his generation, but had become a 'nit picker' and was apt to be a bully, for reasons unknown. My position was peculiar: Setu White and Schultze Keily, Adjutant and Quartermaster respectively, were five and a half and five years senior to me and there were only two officers in this large gap, both absent from the Battalion, McGill in Burma and and Ken Boome on a year's language study in Riga followed by long leave. As both Setu's and Schultze's appointments would terminate shortly, it seemed a foregone conclusion that Strangler Watson and I would in due course fill them, the only other subalterns being 2nd Lieutenants Young and Maguire. This meant that the year that I commanded B Company as a 2nd Lieutenant would be the only time in my regimental career that I commanded a rifle company. From now on it would my fate to be Quartermaster or Adjutant, officiating or permanent, right up up to the time in 1941 when I left to take up appointments in Intelligence.

CHAPTER X

1937 – Signals Officer, Quartermaster and Adjutant

Chemical Warfare and Musketry Courses – 1937–8

MY RECORD OF SERVICE shows me at Regimental Duty (Signals Officer) up to 10th November 1938, then:

Officiating Adjutant – 11th November 1938 to 26th February 1939
Quartermaster   – 26th February 1939 to 24th July 1939
Officiating Adjutant – 25th July 1939 to 29th September 1939

when I reverted to my substantive appointment of Quartermaster, but during this period, I was absent on leave for two months in May and June 1939, and absent on a Command Intelligence Course in March of that year; how did this equate with my holding the appointments of Adjutant or Quartermaster?

There were four regimental appointments which qualified for Extra Duty pay – Commandant, 2nd in Command, Adjutant and Quartermaster, and such appointments were notified in Battalion Part II Orders and entered in the recipient's Record of Service. Regulations stated that Privilege Leave, whether combined with furlough or not, attendance at Courses and certain types of extra regimental employment were classified as regimental duty and the officer concerned did not lose his ED pay. As there could be only one recipient, the officer actually doing the job in such cases was acting, not officiating, and thus received no ED pay and was shown as on 'regimental duty' in his Record of Service.

During the winter of 1937–8 and during most of 1938, I was often acting Adjutant or acting Quartermaster, when either Setu White or Schultze Keily were on leave, so that when I was appointed officiating Adjutant in November, I was fully experienced in both jobs.

On my return from leave, I discovered that the Subedar Major,

Shamshere Mall, had been appointed an Honorary Lieutenant — this was a great honour and from henceforth he would be addressed as 'Lieutenant Sahib' by all ranks, including British officers. Technically he was entitled to wear the same uniform as them, and to use the Officers' Mess; things however did not quite work out like that. The strict dietary rules of the Nepal Durbar precluded the use of the Mess, and the only difference in uniform was the wearing of a tunic with a turn down collar and a collar and tie, instead of that with a high collar worn by Gurkha officers.

Shamshere Mall was due to retire at the end of the year and there was considerable speculation as to his successor. There were two obvious choices — Dhanraj Karki of B Company and Dhanraj Mall of D. Naturally Strangler Watson and I were in favour of Dhanraj Karki and Widdicombe of D Company of Dhanraj Mall, who was his senior Subedar. Mall was the younger and probably the more efficient, but Karki had the better manners and was more respected by the other Gurkha officers. The matter resolved itself when marching out to camp that autumn. The two Gurkha officers were commanding their respective companies which, on account of dust, were marching at ten minute intervals. D Company kept perfect time, but B began to lag behind and at one hourly halt had lost over five minutes. It was obvious that Karki was not sufficiently fit to stand up to a fifteen mile march — so that was that. He went on a well earned pension and Dhanraj Mall became Subedar Major. That this was the correct decision was shown by the fact that he later became Subedar Major of the Regimental Centre and retired after the War as an Honorary Captain.

Shortly after I had returned from leave, I was detailed to attend a Chemical Warfare Course at Belgaum; the Regiment had been ordered to send an officer as there was no one in Dehra qualified to act as Brigade Gas Officer. This was a course that I enjoyed — it was short, only three weeks and except for the part to do with the inspection and fitting of respirators was not so hidebound as other Courses and students were encouraged to think for themselves. Belgaum was south of Bombay and not very far from the sea. Two or three of us hired a car and took a weekend, bathing at a place called Karwar, staying at a small Goanese owned hotel on the beach — I think that we were the only guests. We were advised to hire a boat to take us out to a small island in the bay, where there was a sandy beach. After bathing and sun bathing, we were very reluctant to return for lunch, so we sent the boatman in with a note asking the hotel to send out beer and sandwiches. We got the beer, but instead of the sandwiches came the hotel staff, who cooked and served a magnificent curry on the spot.

I learnt a number of interesting facts. One was that the United States had never adhered to the Treaty outlawing gas. They considered that the use of mustard gas was a cheap and effective way of denying ground to the enemy and was humane as this gas was not a killer. This led me to think of the German tactics in their 1918 offensive when, with the use of gas shells, they had flooded with mustard gas every railway and road junction behind the Allied lines, effectively preventing the reinforcement of the front line. We were required, at the end of the course, to write an essay on any aspect of Chemical Warfare. I used my knowledge of the Indian Railway system to show the possible effect of mustard gas on Indian mobilization to counter a threat through Afghanistan into the North West Frontier Province. The mobilization plan envisaged reinforcement by rail and all movement from east and south would have to pass through either Saharanpur or the triangular junction south of Delhi station. If the enemy was able to saturate these two junctions with mustard gas bombs, no reinforcement of the troops on the frontier could be made. This earned me a good report.

On my return, the normal winter routine was in full swing, but owing to financial stringency only Brigade training was carried out from camp, so I was able to get in a lot of polo. The present British HPA system of handicapping, starting at −2, had its origins in India in 1937, when the IPA considered that mounted units had an unfair advantage over others. Officers of horsed cavalry and artillery in particular could hire unit horses and also had the services of the regimental rough riders to train them; further a 0 handicap could be anything from a beginner to a player of a year or two's experience. Under the new rules mounted units' handicaps started at 0, but for others the lowest was −3. The only grumble was from the Engineers, who had a number of officers in non mounted static appointments, such as Garrison Engineers, but who were classified as belonging to a mounted corps.

The 9th had only two regular players at this time – Tom Scott at 2 and myself at 0, but things changed in the 1938/9 season, as the 1st Battalion returned from their frontier tour with several officers playing and one or two senior officers of the 2/9th such as Walter Fawcett and Billy Fagan returned for short spells between staff jobs; this allowed us to mount a regimental team and sometimes two for the local tournaments. I was rehandicapped locally as a 1 in the spring of 1939 and an IPA 1 in November after my polo career, because of the war and a move, had come to an end.

Battalion and Brigade Training was not very pleasant; as Signals Officer, I was also assistant to Setu White in Battalion HQ. He was nearing the end of his Adjutancy, and was looking forward to a change; furthermore, he did not get on with Bertie Nepean. It was not a happy team in HQ. The CO did not help as he would not make up his mind as to who would be the next Adjutant. Ken Boome put 'the cat among the pigeons' by applying for long leave to commence on conclusion of his study period in Riga. I think Bertie was wrong in granting this; there was no doubt that he was at the top of the roster for 1939, but he had been absent in Europe on study leave for the whole of 1938, as well as being away attached to Army HQ for language study in late 1937.

I found later when I was his Adjutant that despite his bluster, Bertie was a kind hearted person, and of the highest integrity. However, he had two crosses to bear: one was his wife's ardent belief in Moseley and the Fascist cause, the other his fear of having to retire at the end of his period of command; he had never been to the Staff College and at that time few commanding officers achieved full colonel or brigadier without the magic letters 'psc' after their names. Bertie had no private means and promotion would make a great improvement to his financial position. He was determined therefore never to put a foot wrong nor to get involved in anything controversial.

January 1938 saw me on the move again, this time to the Musketry Course at the Pachmarhi Wing of the Small Arms School. I did not want to go on this Course, but it was considered an essential qualification for an Adjutant, a throwback to the days when he was responsible for training the recruits, and Bertie was keen that I should be qualified. The Course was very like the Signals Course – a great deal of unimaginative teaching and learning by rote. I had traded in my V8 and in its place had acquired a big six cylinder Chrysler – it so happened that a school friend of mine, George Field, was serving with the Leicestershire Regiment at Jubbulpore and if I motored down, I could divert there and spend a few days with him. It was a most interesting journey, particularly as the roads once south of Jhansi were only just passable and many of the rivers unbridged, manual ferries being the norm. Two of the Leicesters' subalterns, Patrick Burden and Arthur Denaro, were to attend the Course so I offered them a lift with the proviso that they must send their kit by train together with my bearer Ayoub. Arthur Denaro undertook to make the arrangements, and without my knowledge bought III class tickets for the three bearers and installed them and the kit in a I class compartment; of course, this was objected to by the ticket collector. It was unfortunate that my bearer should have acted as spokesman with all the insolence of a high class Mussulman from the Punjab; this involved me in some unpleasantness with the railway authorities.

The possession of a car made all the difference, as I could get to and from the Field Firing Areas without having to wait for the school transport; naturally, I lifted some of my syndicate. One day, a fellow student, Percy Purcell of the 3rd Gurkhas, not in my syndicate, asked for a lift as he wanted to get back urgently. He was a very small officer, so, as the car was full, we packed him into the boot. I was asked to join a shooting party for the long weekend break; I think this was to provide the transport as I was a rotten shot at birds. The Forest Department produced a forest block, which we heard was one of the best in the vicinity, but very little game materialized. We discovered later that it had been shot over by the Governor only a month before. I offered Percy Purcell a lift back as far as Delhi, which he accepted and we had an uneventful trip, except that I contracted jaundice, which put me in hospital on my return to Dehra.

I think that it was in this summer that the major reorganization of units took place – I may be wrong; it could have been in 1939. It might have been called the 'fours into threes' reorganization – three

Brigades in a Division instead of four, three Battalions in a Brigade and so on. Marching in 'fours' was done away with; in future troops would fall in in three ranks so a simple 'right or left turn' would set them marching in 'threes'. Instead of four companies, A, B, C, and D in a battalion of which one, usually D but C in the 2/9th, was the Machine Gun Company, there would be three Rifle Companies and a Support Company. The new company would have in addition to the MMGs, a Mortar and an Anti Tank Platoon although the formation of these was still in the distant future. HQ Company remained consisting of Battalion HQ, the Signal Platoon and the QM's ragtag and bobtail. One good thing was that the horrible Lewis gun had been replaced by the Vickers-Berthier, the equivalent of the British Army's Bren as the platoon LMG, but at this time carried on a mule. The introduction of a new weapon meant that the Gurkha soldier had to learn a whole lot of new part names which he, as usual, mis-pronounced. Thus the 'flash eliminator' became the 'fish eli-mintor'.

It so happened that while we were struggling to reorganize ourselves, the Army Commander, still 'Dolly' Baird, turned up and demanded to see a Battalion laid out on parade in the new organization; as it was the leave season, neither the newly returned 1st Battalion nor ourselves could produce a full muster so it was decided to mount a composite unit made up from the two battalions. Ted Russel, the 1st Battalion's Adjutant, would be the Adjutant and I the Quartermaster. I was nearly caught out – on seeing the bootmakers, Dolly asked where they were trained and I, chancing my arm, replied, 'Army Clothing Factory, Shahjehanpur, Sir.' The old stinker asked one of the men but luckily he had done a course there.

The UP Government's Circuit House, usually known as Doon Court, was exceptionally well situated and more than usually comfortable, so it attracted many highly placed visitors. The Viceroy made a point of staying there for ten days twice a year while the Government of India's hill moves were taking place; this placed considerable responsibility on the Gurkha Battalions in Dehra, the provision of guards being the main chore, but there were others such as the provision of Bandsmen or Pipers to play at dinner and a Fire Fighting squad. I do not think that the latter would have achieved much with their antique manual pump. Dolly Baird did not endear himself to our Pipers as, although I suggested that he gave them rum after they had played, he offered them lemonade which they refused.

The Government of India in this summer produced the 'free charger scheme': in future mounted officers would be provided with government animals, but the officer would continue to employ and pay the *syce* against the allowance of Rs 15 a month. To implement the scheme a mixed Committee of Veterinary and Remount Officers visited units to assess whether the existing chargers were suitable for Government purchase. As far as I was concerned, I had not put Grave Lady on the strength, although with Bertie's permission, I did try her out on a Battalion ceremonial parade on the polo ground. This was a disaster, as as soon as the troops presented arms, she was away and I could only stop her when we reached the side of the ground, where Joan was waiting for me to change on to. Joan was too old to be taken over so I now had two private ponies. The 9th were lucky in that two of our officers had gone to Remounts, Brian Humphreys and Dick Lovett, so we were assured of really good chargers. I got a three quarter bred gelding trained to stick and ball. As we did a crash move in September 1939, I did not play a great deal of polo on him, but I hunted him regularly with the Peshawar Vale Hunt in 1940.

Now that I had three horses, I thought it time to employ a *daffadar* to oversee the stable. I was able to get a Sikh pensioner, Punjab Singh, who had done the long NCOs' Course at the Saugor Equitation School. He was a good horseman and a first class trainer of polo ponies; furthermore he had a driving licence so he could double as my driver in an emergency. He served me very well up to January 1941 when I left the Battalion. His only fault was that he had a high idea of his own importance, as had many Sikhs. When I engaged him, he made it clear that on no account would he do the work of a *syce* — there must be a *syce* for each horse. Matters came to a head that winter when Schultre Keily and I decided to go to a Christmas camp at Tip. I thought it would be fun if we took a couple of horses down by train with us. Punjab Singh also wished to come to which I agreed but it seemed ridiculous to take two *syces* for three or four days very light work, and in any case with two horses only two men could travel free in the horse box, the third would have to be paid for. Punjab Singh thought otherwise and told me on no account would he look after a horse and completely rejected my explanation that one *syce* would easily do two horses. We parted somewhat in anger but later my bearer came and said, 'Daffadar Ji is outside and wishes to speak to you.' I went out and Punjab Singh went off at the trot to the effect the Sahib had been very angry, very hot, and had said many shameful words, but now the Sahib had cooled, he would see the justice of what he, Punjab Singh, had said, and would do what was right – of course if I wanted to retain him in my service, I had to climb down and order two *syces* to come with us. I must admit that, except for this, he was extremely efficient and hardworking; when we got a 9th team together, he schooled the ponies of the other members as well as mine.

I decided to fly home on short leave in the summer; but this very nearly did not come off – the Fakir of Ipi had set the Frontier ablaze and the Dehra Dun Brigade was first reserve for frontier reinforcement. I was on tenterhooks but luckily the unit selected was from the 2nd Gurkhas, and I got away safely. I travelled by the Imperial Airways Flying Boat service from Gwalior to Southampton which stopped for the night at Dubai, Alexandria and Rome, arriving at Southampton in the afternoon of the fourth day, from whence a special train took passengers to London.

This was quite an exciting trip. Shortly after take off a gentleman introduced himself as Ivor Jehu of the *Times of India*, later to become a war time Brigadier and Director of Public Relations; he explained that he had been asked to look after Lady Bradbourne, the wife of the Governor of Bengal, during the various stopovers and would I team up with him. She was a charming person but regrettably only at Rome were we able to do some sightseeing, taking a horse drawn carriage round the town. The other excitement occurred at Jiwani, the refuelling stop on the Baluchistan coast west of Karachi. A stiff breeze was blowing, and during the manoeuvres to hook the mooring buoy, the boathook was broken and it took about an hour to moor up. The Captain explained that we should have to spend the night there as there were no night landing facilities at Dubai. Jiwani was little more than a sea lagoon and at that time was an enclave of the state of Oman. There was no Imperial Airways Rest House, merely a hut on the beach; the station manager and his wife rose to the occasion and turned up with camp beds, whisky and their cook who prepared sausages and mash for our dinner – this was quite possible as there were only about a dozen passengers and five crew. Naturally when we took off on the following morning, we were well behind schedule and unlikely to reach our night stop at Alexandria before midnight. The Captain gave us the choice of going on or staying the night at Tiberias as he could make up time the following day on the short hop to Rome. We landed at Tiberias in what seemed to be a volley of gun fire, and were greeted by two members of the Palestine gendarmerie, armed to the teeth, who vetoed our night stop as unsafe; this was the time of the Arab Revolt – so on we had to go. The rest of the flight was uneventful and we arrived at Southampton on schedule.

My leave was highlighted by my engagement to Beryl Kavanagh, with marriage in England settled for the following summer, always supposing that I could get leave. The Battalion's future for the next two or three years appeared to have been settled. In normal circumstances, we should begin our two year frontier tour in the spring of 1939, relieving another Gurkha Battalion; it had been decided, however, that the few British battalions on the frontier would be replaced by Gurkhas, and we would replace the South Wales Borderers in the Khyber when their tour ended in spring 1940. It seemed that Beryl and I would have the winter of 1939–40 together in Dehra and I would be due for long leave in 1940. The War however put paid to this, and the separation which it caused was a major factor in the break-up of our marriage.

I returned from leave by air not long before the Munich crisis. Bertie had still not made up his mind about the Adjutancy. Whatever my Record of Service stated I remember that I was Adjutant, acting or officiating, from my return from leave until our move out of Dehra in September 1939. I think Bertie had an idea that if he made Ken Boome Adjutant, he might inveigle him back to the Battalion, and, further, in my case, he was not happy in having a married Adjutant. Although I would not be eligible for promotion to Captain for another five years, I was keen to get the Promotion examination behind me, so I put in to take the written part in October and the practical in the spring of 1939. Meanwhile the Munich crisis was fast approaching and also I found it impossible to study while I was Adjutant, so I persuaded Bertie to allow me ten days casual leave and I departed to Simla with a borrowed copy of Pitman's correspondence course. The actual Munich detente came the day that I arrived there, and there was no doubt of the relief shown by everyone. On my return, I took the exam and passed.

Collective training took the form of Frontier Warfare in the foothills of the Doon Valley. While the drills could be practised, everything else was rather artificial as the heavily wooded Dehra hills were quite unlike the arid frontier terrain. The officer situation had changed completely as my original friends, Widdy, Setu and Shultze, had left and been replaced by Strangler Watson, Leslie Young and Maggie Maguire. Strangler and I were firm friends and we made a good team as Adjutant and Quartermaster respectively, I hope as good a team as our predecessors, Setu and Schultze, but I was never very intimate with Leslie or Maguire. 'AO' Robinson had departed to the Staff College, but the unflappable John Hudson was still with the Machine Guns. The three senior officers, Bertie, Tom Scott and Nick Hurst, were not particularly close. I got into trouble with Nick, whom I disliked and he disliked me; he was acting CO on a Brigade frontier exercise and the Brigadier, who knew nothing about the frontier, wished to see how the troops bedded down at night in a defended camp. Normally at dusk 'stand-to' everyone took up their night defensive positions, but for the Brigadier's edification, in this case, all but the night duty personnel would lie down in their bivouacs, and on a second order would take up their stand-to positions. This was altogether too much for the Gurkha brain and on 'Stand-to' utter chaos reigned, half of the troops standing-to and half lying down. The Brigadier was furious. I tried to explain that the Gurkha soldier had had the meaning of stand-to drilled into him and it was difficult to explain another meaning. I am afraid this made matters worse and infuriated Nick who gave me good bawling out. This did me no harm as Nick was only acting as CO and I was both by seniority and as Adjutant immune from his unpleasant attitudes.

CHAPTER XI

1939 – A Momentous Year: Marriage and the Outbreak of War

Command Intelligence Course – Watson, the Quartermaster, killed by a tiger and a crash move to Nowshera

THERE WERE THREE events in 1939, which had a bearing on my career – marriage, the Eastern Command Intelligence Course, and the outbreak of War. I had got my leave sanctioned for May and June and the wedding was scheduled for late May at St Paul's, Knightsbridge; George Bolton of the 1st Battalion would be my best man. The intention was to fly home, but to return by ship as we should have a great deal of household gear with us.

Bertie Nepean had intimated that he did not disapprove of my marriage, as I had sufficient private means to support a wife 'off the strength'. He was still unhappy with the idea of a married Adjutant, and with the idea of inveigling Ken Boome back to the Battalion, made him Adjutant *in absentia*, and I the Quartermaster, officiating Adjutant and drawing the allowance; Strangler Watson then becoming the officiating Quartermaster.

I had, however, another iron in the fire; it was not unusual for subalterns of five or six years service to go off on secondment for three or four years to one of the Frontier Corps, the Assam Rifles, the Burma Military Police or as an Air Intelligence Liaison Officer with the RAF on the North West Frontier. My preference was for the last, but there was a snag – prior attendance at a Command Intelligence Course for which the minimum service qualification was seven years, and I had only five. It so happened, that I had been approached by a GSO II at District HQ, Bill Oliver, for the appointment of ADC to the new Commander, Auchinleck; an offer withdrawn when he learned that I was getting married. He offered his good offices, however, to try and get me a place on a Course starting in Bareilly on 23rd March.

So far so good, but, as usual, another snag occurred. As I said earlier I had passed the written part of my promotion examination the previous autumn – now, out of the blue came an order to report at Delhi to take the practical part on the 23rd and 24th March, a Monday and a Tuesday; obviously I could not be in two places on the same day. However, Bill Oliver made some enquiries of HQ Eastern Command, who said that if I could arrive in time to start work on Thursday morning, I would be accepted. Troubles never come singly. I had found the Chrysler very expensive to run and with the expenses of a married establishment in view, had traded it in for a new Ford 10. This had begun to 'pink' very badly, so on my arrival at Delhi, I took it to the Ford agents who diagnosed excess carbon, probably due to adulterated petrol. They agreed to take off the cylinder head, do a 'decoke' and have the car ready by Tuesday evening for me to drive to Bareilly on Wednesday. Unfortunately, they did not run the car for a while and then tighten the cylinder head nuts: the result, I had only gone about thirty miles beyond Meerut when the gasket blew. I managed to get the car back to a garage there, but in order to get to the Course on time had to abandon it and continue by train.

It seems incredible today that although my final appointment in Intelligence was Chief Intelligence Officer of a Command the size of France and Benelux put together, my formal instruction was only the nine days of this Course; the rest consisted of the rules and procedures which I made up as I went along. I cannot say that either the Course or my fellow students were very inspiring as Intelligence was very much of backwater at that time. The Course tried to squeeze too much into too short a time – Military Intelligence in War, Air Photo Interpretation, Internal Security, Indian Political Intelligence, all in twelve working days. I remember one particular exercise, probably because I was the Syndicate Leader. We were sent to prepare an Internal Security Report on a nearby District, Budaon, and the Chief Instructor had decreed that none of the District Staff should speak to us in English. They were all Indians and obeyed their instructions to the letter. The other members of my Syndicate were British Service Officers, with little or no knowledge of Urdu, so the bulk of the work fell on me. I was rewarded, when six years later, as Chief Intelligence

Officer of Central Command, I found that our report was still the standard work on the District.

My course results exceeded all my expectations; I passed out top and was recommended for a variety of Intelligence appointments, ranging from a GSO III (Intelligence) in war, through an AILO with the RAF to Indian Political Intelligence. My preference had veered away from being an AILO to Civil Intelligence and appointment as a 'Military Intelligence Officer' with the Intelligence Bureau of the Government of India. The Intelligence Bureau was India's MI5 and MI6 combined and MIOs were seconded to the Civil Police in difficult or disturbed areas, where they acted as Field Agents of the IB and as a liaison between the military and the police to which end they were granted the ex officio rank of Additional Superintendent of Police. The final remarks on my report read, 'He desires training for employment as an MIO and should be attached to Army HQ for that purpose.' It looked as if I had got what I wanted, but in fact things turned out differently. I never got the attachment to Army HQ, nor the post of MIO and it was eighteen months before I received any Intelligence appointment.

Between the course and proceeding on leave, I was invited to join a team for the annual Roorkee Polo week. The team, 'Gurkhalry', consisted of two 9th Gurkhas, Noel George and myself, and two cavalrymen, Hugh McKillop of the Scinde Horse and Jimmy Gimson of the Guides Cavalry. Roorkee, 42 miles from Dehra on the Delhi road, was not a town in the ordinary sense, but merely a small cantonment containing the HQ of the King George's Own Bengal Sappers and Miners, the UP Government's Irrigation Department and the Thomason College. It had been founded in the early 1850s for the construction of the Ganges Canal, the first of the great north Indian irrigation works. The canal started from a headworks near the holy city of Hardwar to flow finally into the Jumna east of Delhi. After the Great War, the falls on the canal were utilised to generate electricity to power the individual pumps for the 'tube well' irrigation scheme. The Thomason College was built at the same time as the canal to train Indians as 'chain men' and to fill junior supervisory and clerical posts in the canal service. It was enlarged after Independence to become the University of Roorkee.

Bertie Nepean very kindly lent me his pony for the tournament but refused me casual leave – this put me under a considerable strain, as I had to motor down and back for each day of the tournament. The ponies were walked down by easy stages, under the supervision of Punjab Singh. We won our first match and then came up against the 2nd Gurkhas in the semi final. Theirs was the team which won the all India Infantry Cup that year. It was a fast and furious game which we only just lost. Poor Grave Lady had to play two very fast chukkers, and was very lame after them, so I had to send her home by train. We then passed into the subsidiary tournament, which we won easily. I think that because of the War this was the last tournament that I was to play in.

At long last Bertie had been forced to make up his mind over the Adjutancy as Army HQ had intimated that, on the conclusion of his leave, Ken Boome would be seconded to their Interpreter branch, and thus come off the regimental list. He was prepared now to have me as a married Adjutant, but the formal appointment must wait until Boome was off our books; at the same time Strangler would become permanent Quartermaster. He, in the meantime, had gone off on leave to shoot in the CP jungles. Shortly before I was due to leave for England came a telegram from the British Military Hospital, Jubbulpore, saying that he had been admitted after having been mauled by a tiger.

As I was due to fly off from Gwalior in a few days time Bertie told me to leave immediately for Jubbulpore, find out how serious Strangler's injuries were, and having posted a report, return to Gwalior and catch my plane home – the Battalion would refund my extra expenses. I found him looking very well and cheerful, but the prognosis was very bad. He had been bitten through the fleshy part of the thigh and gangrene had set in. Matters were not helped in that it had taken some eight hours to get him by bullock cart to the Mission Hospital at Itarsi for emergency treatment and another twelve to transfer him by train to Jubbulpore. Although he put up a gallant fight, he died about three weeks later. Had there been penicillin, or even sulfa drugs, he probably would have survived. He was buried in the Cantonment Cemetery where his grave, still in good condition, was visited in 1996 by his niece. The full circumstances of the incident have remained obscure, probably because the *shikari* and forest guard who were present were frightened of blame, but it seems that the tiger came out during a bird beat and Strangler had only a shot gun, his rifle being carried by the *shikari*.

Once again I was uncertain if I would get my leave; this time it was the international situation. Germany had annexed the rump of Czechoslovakia without any overt action from Britain or France, but now Italy had invaded Albania and we had to land at Brindisi and Rome on the way home. Nothing in fact happened, but all of us on the plane were hoping that we would get past Rome as then we could only go on. The night stop had been altered to Marseilles, but we still had to refuel at Rome. At one time it looked if we would be stuck there as our pilot made a bad landing at Lake Bracciano, and only a sharp turn stopped us running aground.

Our wedding took place as planned and we had our honeymoon at Chagford on Dartmoor. For our return we decided not to utilise the P & O Express but to spend a couple of days in Paris. This was facilitated by the introduction of two new trains: the sleeping car 'Night Ferry' leaving London at 9 pm and reaching Paris the next morning and the 'Train Aerodynamic', the predecessor of the famous 'Mistral', which left Paris at noon and arrived at Marseilles at 9.15 pm, the boat not leaving until midnight. The *Mooltan*, on which we travelled, was one of the largest P & Os, 21,000 tons, but by no means one of the best; she did not have the more modern 'Thermotank' ventilation, but only electric fans, her electrical equipment was constantly giving trouble and finally she did not keep time, arriving at midnight on the Thursday compelling us to take Friday's 'Frontier Mail'. I was lucky as the Embarkation Staff selected me to escort three bags of confidential documents as far as Delhi, for which Government paid my fare.

We had been allotted No 8 Bungalow, one of the farther ones backing on to the forest, but John Hudson, who was temporarily absent, lent us his, No 7, while we were getting ours ready. I soon found out that two jobs had come my way while I was on leave but Bertie had refused both of them on my behalf. One was MIO Eastern States at Ranchi, and the other Assistant Commandant of the new paramilitary Crown Representative's Police being raised at Neemuch.

To support his actions to Higher Authority, he had said that I was indispensable as Adjutant in view of the international situation.

Beryl and I settled down to the not very pleasant period of the end of the hot weather and the onset of the rains; there was little social life as most of the wives had gone up to Mussoorie. Poor Sally had died while I was on long leave in 1937 and I now had a large black Labrador, which we used to take swimming in the Tons river and the adjacent small canals. However, as Adjutant, I had plenty of work, particularly as we had both a Test Mobilization and an Internal Security Exercise. The latter caused me some problems – in the 9th, officers did not require any special permission to leave the station or even to be absent overnight at weekends or other holidays; this meant that in the event of an emergency call-out, I would have no idea of the whereabouts of some of the officers. Bertie agreed with me so I issued an order requiring officers leaving the station to record their names and whereabouts in a book in my office. This brought me into collision with Leslie Young as Bertie, casually perusing the book, considered that Leslie was spending too much time in Mussoorie. The 2nd Gurkhas required their subalterns to obtain permission to go there and even put one Hotel, Hackmans, out of bounds, but we in the 9th had more trust in our junior officers. Leslie failed to take the hint so was given a direct order, which he twice disobeyed; most COs would have got rid of him, but he stayed. Another headache was Tom Scott's habitual unpunctuality. On a ceremonial parade he was required to call the Battalion to attention when the CO rode on. I was always worried that he was not going to make it in time and one awful day he did not, arriving on parade after Bertie, who was furious. As a result, Bertie ordered me to go personally to Tom's bungalow thirty minutes before parade and stay with him until I was satisfied that he would be dressed and on parade on time – this was an order that I conveniently failed to carry out.

The outbreak of the War made very little impact as India did not mobilize; further, it had been expected ever since the Hitler–Stalin Pact so the actual Declaration was somewhat of an anticlimax; routine continued as usual. As our move to the Khyber was now only four or five months away, Bertie obtained sanction for a special advance party of the QMJ, two other GOs and myself to go to Landi Kotal and spy out the land; this would be facilitated as there was a Gurkha Battalion already there, the 2/5 RGR, with whom the GOs could stay. With my bearer and the GO's orderlies this made a party of seven. Government did not pay 'Mail' train fares for GOs and GORs so it meant a very slow journey. Bertie agreed that we could take the regimental bus to Saharanpur to pick up the Delhi–Peshawar all stations passenger, even so a train journey of about forty hours. This was no hardship for me as I enjoyed train travel; the Guard wired ahead for my meals which were brought to my compartment and the rest of the party fed from the station food stalls. I was not able to see the famous Khyber Railway as we were lifted to and from Peshawar by lorry. While I was away Beryl went to stay with friends in Mussoorie.

On the conclusion of our visit we returned to find all in confusion – orders had come that the Battalion was to leave for Nowshera in five days time to replace the 1st Dorsets who had gone to the Middle East. This produced a number of problems. The first was the availability of officers – we had present in order of seniority the CO, Tom Scott second in command, Nick Hurst recruit company commander, John Hudson attached to Brigade HQ as Station Staff Officer, myself officiating Adjutant, Leslie Young, Maguire officiating QM and two newly joined second lieutenants, Ridout and Buchanan. Gurkha Regiments had no training battalions, but each battalion had its own recruit training company which when the unit was absent from its home station formed the Depot.

On top of everything else came a signal ordering Bertie to report to Army HQ forthwith for employment with the Gwalior State Forces – he would be replaced by Walter Fawcett returning from the IDC in England. Tom Scott had already left with the advance party, Nick would stay behind as Depot Commander and John Hudson would remain as SSO; this meant that the command of the Battalion would devolve on me, a Lieutenant of only five years service assisted by two experienced subalterns and two just joined. At this point, Nick, terrified that he lose the job of Depot Commander and be ordered to rejoin the Battalion, sent a written order to John Hudson to return immediately; he had no authority to do this and John Hudson showed it to the Brigadier, who was not pleased.

The next problem was what the Battalion should take with them – our orders specified that we were moving 'in relief' as our sojourn in Nowshera would be brief and we would move on to Landi Kotal in due course. To save transport charges units moving 'in relief' left behind most of their warlike stores and took over those of the unit they relieved. Thus we would leave behind our first line ammunition and our MMG and LMG mules. This was going to cause problems on arrival at Nowshera. The final problem was Beryl and the disposal of our household gear – our move orders made no mention of the move of officers' families; this only affected me as I was the only married officer going. In view of the uncertainty of married accommodation and the short time to pack up, it seemed wiser for her to stay put and come on later when the situation clarified. The car would remain with her – officers' chargers would go with us so that took care of one horse; an Indian railway horsebox accommodated six horses and regulations stated that any spare spaces could be offered free to officers in order of juniority so I was assured of places for Grave Lady and Joan.

The Battalion was given a good send off; the 1st Battalion lining the road out of Birpur. Bertie, almost in tears, led the march to the station. I would have liked to have been marching behind him as Adjutant, but it had been decided that Maggie Maguire had not the experience necessary to outwit the Railway's probable attempts to catch us out over dilapidated rolling stock, so I proceeded direct to the station to take over the train assisted by Maggie; Leslie acting as Adjutant.

It is sad to think that the Battalion never marched back at the end of the War, as it was captured at Singapore. The present 2nd Battalion was formed in 1946 from the 5th Battalion to which a few men from the Japanese Prisoner of War camps were added.

CHAPTER XII

Winter 1939–40
– Nowshera and Landi Kotal

Back to Quartermaster, Separation – Beryl sets up house in Peshewar

OUR JOURNEY TO Nowshera was uneventful, but not very pleasant – although we were on 'hot weather fast timings' we were still two nights *en route*. We arrived at Lahore on a very hot and sticky evening for a long meal halt, and I persuaded the station authorities to turn on the carriage watering taps above the BO and GOs' carriages, which cooled them down considerably. I would have liked to have done the same for the troops, but I was uncertain how waterproof their window shutters were.

Nowshera was situated on the plain of the Kabul river about 30 miles from Peshawar by rail and road. It was the Headquarters of a Frontier Brigade designed to back up the garrisons in the tribal territory of the Malakand; immediately to the north were the cantonments of Risalpur and Mardan, the former containing the 1st (Risalpur) Cavalry Brigade, and the latter famous as the original home of the legendary Corps of Guides and the starting point of their famous march to Delhi in 1857. The Cantonment was bisected by the railway line; the smaller portion to the south contained the British Infantry Lines which we would occupy, while the northern portion had the other units, Brigade HQ, the Hotel and the Club.

Tom Scott decided that I should continue as QM until the Battalion had fully settled in; this was going to take longer than anticipated owing to the bureaucratic red tape of the MES. The British barracks were furnished with 'Cots BT' while we were entitled only to 'Charpoys IT': much time being wasted in returning the one and drawing the other. A large modern two story barrack with amenity rooms on the ground floor and accommodation for HQ Company above was locked and the MES refused to open it as

Gurkha soldiers were not entitled to such amenities, and, anyway, the building was full of the furniture and stores of the Dorset's contractor. Indenting for and drawing 1st Line ammunition was another time wasting chore — the mule problem was solved by sending a party of muleteers up to Landi Kotal to take over and walk down the SWB's mules. We were lucky in having a top rate Brigade Commander in Archie Nye, later Deputy CIGS and the last British Governor of Madras. The Staff Captain was a KCIO Captain Thakur Nathu Singh, who was destined to become the first Indian Colonel of the 9th Gurkhas.

Not long after we arrived the QMJ complained of the rice issued by the local Supply Depot; I had a look at it and saw instead of the long grained, white rice to which we were accustomed in Dehra, this was small grained, brown and broken. The Supply Officer maintained that the rice was up to specification and considered that our complaint was frivolous. However, when he realised that we had come from Dehra, he burst out laughing saying that his was Kashmiri contract rice and we could no longer expect locally purchased Basmati. Today any good rice, wherever grown, is often classified as Basmati, but genuine Basmati was then only grown in the Doon Valley.

Our officer structure had changed considerably — but not to my advantage. Walter Fawcett and Sid de Wilton joined from the UK. The former was an exceptionally brilliant officer; he had been both a Brevet Major and a Brevet Lieutenant Colonel, an Instructor at the Staff College and had just completed the IDC Course; on the other hand, he had been away from regimental duty for so long that he was out of touch with the present battalion — indeed the only officers with whom he had served were Tom Scott and Nick Hurst. One of his first acts was to confirm me as QM and to get John Hudson back to be Adjutant. He explained that, since Strangler's death, there was no one else with sufficient 'Q' experience; this was in fact true, but I suspect that he considered that an Adjutant had to be a Captain as was usual when he had last served in the Battalion. As I had been promised the Adjutancy by Bertie Nepean and had been doing the job for most of the year, this was great blow. Meanwhile I secured a room in the Hotel for Beryl and me — she motored up as far as Rawalpindi, escorted by Peter Cane of the 1st Battalion, from whence I fetched her.

We did one or two Battalion exercises to keep our hand in, otherwise our time in Nowshera was generally uneventful. Polo restarted with the advent of the cold weather so I was able to get some station chukkers. There was an episode of black humour involving three almost identical Ford 10s, Sid de Wilton, Leslie Young and myself. The Club laid on a special Charity Dance for Remembrance Day to which most of us went. Sid, who had borrowed Tom Scott's Ford 10, became somewhat 'merry' which came to the notice of Mrs Brigadier, who ordered the 9th to remove their objectionable officer. The task, unfortunately, fell to Leslie as Adjutant as John Hudson had not yet arrived: unfortunately as Leslie was lacking in tact and Sid considered him an upstart young puppy. However after some argument the two of them got into what was thought to be Tom Scott's car, Sid insisting on driving. The car refused to start so I brought up my Ford 10 and gave it a push, bumper to bumper. This did the trick and off they went; I considered it prudent to follow. The level crossing gates were shut and Sid hit them. Getting out to help I was confronted with a scene out of Bedlam – the car with a stuck throttle roaring like a mad beast, Leslie standing in the road holding his nose which had hit the windscreen and exclaiming, 'My nose is broken,' and getting no sympathy from Sid who was repeating, 'Don't be so silly, Leslie, you are not hurt at all.' I got them back into the car, the gates opened and I saw them safely to their destination. Returning to the Club, I picked up Beryl and we went home to bed. The next morning our crimes were revealed – Sid had got into the Brigade Major's car, not Tom's; they were as alike as two peas. Worse, as our bumpers did not coincide, I had smashed the BM's rear light. Naturally a furious letter arrived from Brigade – however, I came out of it reasonably well, as all that was said about me was, 'Mains was the only one who was not drunk.'

The question of Beryl's accommodation in Peshawar while I was in Landi Kotal, a non family station, had to be settled. The usual accommodation was in Army Mansions, a block of bedsits with a communal dining room usually reserved for junior marrieds as it was relatively cheap; only messing charges were levied, although in my case being 'off the strength', room rent less a single lodging allowance would be charged. The alternative was 'Holmes Flats', single storied apartments comprising sitting room, dining room, pantry, double bedroom and bathroom with cookhouse and servants quarters adjacent. They were considerably more expensive as the rent was paid direct to the owner, Holmes the Peshawar photographer, against receipt of the appropriate lodging allowance. They were much in demand by senior officers.

Beryl and I motored up to Peshawar to inspect the bedsit in Army Mansions reserved for us and took an instant dislike to it; as we could afford something better, we rushed off to Holmes and very luckily and unusually, he had a flat vacant, which we took on the spot. This annoyed Walter Fawcett, who considered that we were getting too big for our boots.

Our movement orders duly arrived – including our transport, we were to move by train; this put an additional burden on me as, at that time, the QM was also the Transport Officer. Our horses were no problem; as we would take over three or four line ponies for any mounted duties, we decided to leave them in Peshawar with the 16th Light Cavalry. The two horse boxes would be cut off from our train there and unloaded by Sowars from the 16th. The mules were going to be a real problem; unlike our Dehra mules who had practised loading and unloading into mock up rail wagons and lorry bodies, the SWB mules had been on the Frontier all their working life, and had never even seen a railway wagon. Wooden floored all steel goods wagons with a central door each side were provided, each to contain ten mules, five a side, heads to the centre with only a single transverse rope to hold them. Loading was murder – there was little working space, the mules were fractious, and as soon as one was safely in position, the injection of a second was an invitation for the first to come out, often with flying hoofs. That we achieved our object without serious injuries was largely due to Punjab Singh, who although it was really no business of his, virtually took command.

The Khyber Pass is generally believed to be, and, indeed is often shown on small scale maps as, the frontier between India, as it then was, and Afghanistan, but in fact the actual frontier is on the far side of the Pass on the plain of the Kabul River; the actual watershed is at

Landi Kotal. The entrance is at Jamrud about ten miles from Peshawar, from where the road and railway rise sharply to the Ali Masjid gorge; onwards to Landi Kotal about thirty miles from Peshawar, there is a fairly gentle rise up a wide valley dotted with fortified villages. The descent begins at Landi Kotal, fairly gentle for the two or three miles to Michhni Khandao, then a very steep descent, 1 in 25 on the railway, to Landi Khana the terminus. A mile or so further on is Torhkam, the frontier post. Control gates manned by khassadars at Jamrud and Michhni stopped casual visitors. There were in fact two roads, the well engineered motor road and parallel to it the caravan route. The only branch road was from Michhni to Charbagh Fort which, by a jink of the frontier, lay directly above Torkham. The Pass was in the territory of the Afridis, who policed it with tribal khassadars and received a subsidy to compensate for the tolls which they used to levy on caravans. The whole area was in tribal territory under the Deputy Commissioner, Peshawar acting as Political Agent, Khyber with an APA, at Landi Kotal.

The Landi Kotal Brigade was the largest and probably the most interesting Brigadier's command in India as it consisted of six battalions in eight locations, not counting platoon or section permanent pickets. Landi Kotal had Brigade HQ, a Mountain Battery, AT Company, Hospital, Supply Depot and three battalions, with a two company detachment at Charbagh Fort. Halfway up the Pass was a battalion at Shagai with a detachment at Ali Masjid. Jamrud had a battalion and on the adjacent Khajuri Plain was another battalion and a Mountain Battery, split between Bara Fort, Fort Salop and Jhansi Post, these three latter locations being supplied from Peshawar. The British Battalion did a one year tour entirely in Landi Kotal; the Indian Army units two years, but in different locations. A newly arrived battalion would normally serve the first year on the Khajuri, in Jamrud or Shagai or a combination of two of these locations, before moving up to Landi Kotal for their final year; as we were taking over the role of the British battalion, we moved there direct.

Until 1920 there had been no permanent Regular Army garrison in the Khyber; the three Forts of Jamrud. Ali Masjid and Landi Kotal were manned by the para-military Khyber Rifles, with their HQ at the latter place. They were mainly comprised of Afridis who mutinied in the 3rd Afghan War of 1919, after which it was decided that the defence of the Pass should be taken over by Regulars. The main garrison was originally at Landi Khana, but this place was abandoned for health reasons in 1922 and a new fortified camp built at Landi Kotal. The Khajuri Plain was the traditional winter grazing ground of the Afridi tribes from the Tirah and had been occupied periodically as a a punishment. The decision to garrison it permanently was taken after the Afridi raid on Peshawar Cantonment in 1930.

Landi Kotal was a fortified camp built around the old Khyber Rifles Fort, the site of which housed Brigade HQ, the Brigade Officers' Mess and the Hospital; also in the centre were the Mountain Battery, the AT Company's Lines and a small bazaar. Each battalion was allotted a sector of the perimeter to defend and thus occupied the barrack huts in that area. We were lucky that in our sector was an old fort which had been converted into transport lines, so that the mule stables were hidden away and were no annoyance. We had the same frustrations as in Nowshera, having to change the barrack furniture from that authorised for British troops to that authorised for us. Our Officers' Mess had been built to accommodate thirty or so officers, in which our six or seven were quite lost. The whole camp was surrounded by barbed wire with watchtowers and searchlights at intervals. The gates were closed at Retreat when the night positions were manned. There was a small area on the adjacent landing ground demarcated by white stones which could be used during daylight for games and recreation generally. Outside close by was the railway station and the APA's office, both capable of defence and manned by khassadars. The camp was partially overlooked by surrounding low hills and on these permanent pickets had been built — these were stone towers garrisoned by one or two sections; they were entered at first floor level by a ladder which was drawn up at night. At this time when the area was deemed to be peaceful, half were handed over to the khassadars to garrison.

The Khyber road could be used in the day without an escort. Most officers who had wives in Peshawar were allowed weekend leave, leaving on Saturday after work and in time to pass the Jamrud barrier by 6 pm, returning Monday morning at 6 am to be in time for first parade. When we first arrived, ladies were allowed up to Landi Kotal for lunch on holidays, but this was later stopped for security reasons in connection with the new defences. There was one exception to the daylight rule – Brigadier Hickman, the Brigade Commander, was a keen rider to hounds so he persuaded the APA to have the road picketed by the khassadars from 3 am on days when the Peshawar Vale Hounds met. A curious facet of soldiering on the Frontier was that a pistol was of more value to a tribesman than a dead officer – thus on no account should an officer be armed when going alone outside the camp. If an officer wished to go out on a reconnaissance, an indent would be made on the APA for a khassadar as escort; he would be armed but not his charge.

Individual training and range firing was carried out normally and there was also a certain amount of company and battalion training. Brigade Training took the form of the bi-annual 'columns' designed to 'show the flag'. This was a specialized form of warfare, which I have explained in detail in Appendix D. It would be suicidal to send out a body of troops armed but without ammunition, so to prevent accidents when two bodies of troops were pitted against each other with blank ammunition, special measures were essential. A proportion of riflemen, LMGs and MMGs were armed with live ammunition, identified by red cloth tied round the weapons and riflemen's pouches and covering the boxes of reserve ammunition.

An unpleasant chore was forced upon us as a result of the War and the Hitler–Stalin Pact: the digging of a Defence Line against a Russian advance into India. This was a case of 'all hands to the pumps' as, in addition to the Landi Kotal battalions, those on the Khajuri and in Peshawar were brought in to help. As the ground was hard rock or shale, not a great deal was accomplished. The most bizarre aspect was the anti tank defence – there was not one anti tank gun in India in 1939 but there were in store the Horse Artillery 13 pounders displaced by mechanization. Some bright spark had the idea that if these guns were emplaced and fired over open sights, they might (and I repeat might) stop a Russian tank. Four guns were issued to us and we were ordered to train a platoon, or troop, to fire them. The Mountain Gunners had little knowledge of them and the Battery Commander rudely stated that, if he ever had to take our platoon to practice camp for live firing, he would put in for leave. The training consisted of lining up the four guns on the square in front of the Quarter Guard, when a Gurkha would walk across the front carrying a representation of a tank on a pole, whereupon the gunlayers would keep the target in their sights. One day a layer came to the end of his traverse, so naturally the traversing wheel jammed; a Gurkha was not stopped by so small a matter, so with a grunt the layer gave a mighty heave and the wheel came off in his hand. Not long after, we had a fire practice. The regimental Provost Naik's duty was to turn on the water at the hydrant and all went well until the order to shut down was given, but the water continued to flow. Shouts and yells in English, Urdu and Gurkhali were of no avail as the water went on cascading down the road, until finally the man admitted that he was turning the stopcock the wrong way and had broken the valve – it took the MES two hours to stop the flow and we were very unpopular as we had flooded the bazaar.

The other two units in Landi Kotal were the 2/5th Royal Gurkha Rifles and the 4/15th Punjab Regiment. The former was a first class unit with a first class CO, Cameron, later to command the 48th (all Gurkha) Indian Infantry Brigade with great gallantry on the Burma Retreat; the adjutant, Philip Townsend, was the brother of Peter Townsend of the Princess Margaret affair. The 4/15th was not a particularly good battalion, but they did have a KCIO, 'Jick' Rudra who had served in the Great War in the ranks of the Royal Fusiliers, was wounded and ended the War as a Sergeant. He also had the distinction of being one of only three KCIOs serving in non Indianised units. One of the Khajuri battalions, the 2/12th Frontier Force Regiment (2nd Sikhs), was a fine Regiment who like the 2/9th served in Malaya where a British Officer, Cummins, won a VC. Brigadier Hickman was a pleasant easy-going officer, but we seldom saw him – he was the senior Brigadier in Peshawar District, so whenever the District Commander was absent he was away to Peshawar to answer for him.

This winter was not a particularly happy one either for me or for the Battalion. In the first place Walter Fawcett, while being a very nice person and a brilliant officer, was not a good CO – he had been away too long, and as a result was apt to place too much reliance on the views of the senior officers with whom he had served, even though they too had been away from the Regiment for several years. Matters were made worse by the return from staff employment of Majors and Captains who only stayed for a month or two before going off again and for whom some employment had to be found. If they were given command of Companies they would replace for only a short period subalterns who knew their GOs and men. In order to keep the existing subaltern Company Commanders and to preserve continuity, Walter made the seniors Inspectors of this and that – Training or Administration for example. This was not a wise move as no one knew to whom they were responsible, the CO or the Inspector; further, it interfered with the traditional role of the Adjutant and QM as the CO's personal staff officers. Another difficulty was his frequent absences; he was the senior Lieutenant Colonel in the Brigade and Hickman was the senior Brigadier, so the absence either of the Brigade or District Commander deprived us of our CO.

To my great regret, as I had served with him since I joined in 1935, Tom Scott left to go as a Lieutenant Colonel to be Senior Supervising Officer of the Kalibahadur Regiment of the Royal Nepalese Army and to my further regret Nick arrived as 2 i/c. Other visitors were Steve Steveney, 'AO' Robinson, George Nangle and Malcolm McGill. At the bottom end of the scale we were blessed with an excellent lot of subalterns – Leslie Young, Maggie Maguire and Chris Graham-Hogg were competent officers and of the newcomers, Bill Ridout was quite exceptional and Roland Buchanan had held a TA Commission. Nick proceeded to make himself unpopular. John Hudson with Walter's approval had renewed our Field Service crockery and cutlery which was quite unsuitable for the quasi peace time conditions of Landi Kotal – to this Nick took great exception as irresponsible and extravagant but he got nowhere with John who merely ignored him. He met his match in McGill who was Mess Secretary. He was berating him over the condition of the Anteroom and, in particular, the state of the china globes under the electric lights. Malcolm stood on a chair and to get a better view tipped up the bowl which deposited a collection of dead insects down Nick's shirt front. Nick was not amused.

In the New Year, for what reason I know not, I came to the notice of the Brigade Staff as a bright boy who in due course might be considered for the Staff College. This led to me being appointed Brigade Orderly Officer for the spring Column and subsequently Staff Captain for a month while the incumbent was on leave. I did not relish the former appointment because as a subaltern, I was at the beck and call not only of the Brigadier and the Brigade Staff proper but also of the Brigade Signals and Intelligence Officers. The pitching and striking of the Brigade camp was my responsibility, assisted by the Brigade duty platoon; this was found by a different battalion each day and was an unpopular chore. The platoon, therefore, was often late and in a bolshie frame of mind. On the other hand, I very much enjoyed my month as Staff Captain. One would have thought that a formation of the size and complexity of the Landi Kotal Brigade would have merited a DAA & QMG with a Staff Captain as assistant and a large clerical staff, but on the contrary, there was only the Staff Captain with a clerical staff of three Indian civilian members of the permanent cadre of the IACC – one Upper Division Clerk for 'A' and one Upper and one Lower for 'Q'. Every letter which came in was put up to me with the references duly tagged and a draft suggested reply, the whole tied up on a file board. I am afraid that I had a serious row with Nick who was officiating in Walter's absence. The 2/9th were duty battalion and had received a work order for some routine task and Nick sent me a scribbled note saying that he was not going to obey it – Nick had a habit of writing notes on dog eared dirty bits of paper. This was altogether too much, so wearing my blue staff armband, I marched off to see him. His reaction was to say that as the 2/9th was my battalion, I should let them off lightly. My reply was that he knew very well that I could not do that. An argument ensued, which I brought to a close by reminding him that anything I signed was an order from the Brigadier, so he must make a formal complaint, adding – did he really want me to show his dog eared note to him? This finished it, so with no good grace he gave in and accepted the work order.

My marriage began to run into difficulties – I found that coming down to Peshawar most weekends was probably worse than complete separation. Beryl had a circle of admirers and naturally wanted to beat it up in the Club at weekends, while I was tired and wanted a quiet

Saturday after a week's work. Matters were not helped by Walter trying to organize us at Christmas to which Beryl took great exception. Punjab Singh's driving licence was a great help as Beryl could have the car during the week and he could bring it up for me on Saturdays and take it back on Monday. The Ford 10 was proving too small and Beryl took a dislike to it, so I changed it for a Ford V8 convertible; I became much in demand by married officers for lifts to Peshawar. I started hunting with the PVH after Christmas and took a really bad toss. I had decided to hunt on my official charger, but as I had never jumped him, I thought prudent to try him out in the Cavalry manège; all went well until I was about to go home, when I thought I would try him over a really big jump and in view of its size took it rather fast – disaster, he did not rise an inch, crashed straight into the fence and came down; naturally I came off and he ran his hooves right up my back. Luckily I broke no bones but I was black and blue. Struggling into a stiff shirt and tail coat to go out to dinner that night was agony. It transpired that he was a horse who would jump only when 'collected' and given that, he proved an excellent hunter.

Up to April 1940 the War had passed us by – except for the Khyber Defences, peace time routine continued; we even wore peacetime Mess kit for dinner. As there had been no mobilization, we were continuing to discharge time expired GOs and GORs to pension and replacing them by new enlistments. The folly of this became apparent when India did finally mobilize and these men, with no reserve liability, were lost to us. Our loss was the Royal Nepalese Army's gain – they arrived on a rifle and haversack basis and had to be issued with and trained to use MMGs, LMGs and signalling equipment. A number of our pensioners were taken on – the GOs as officers and senior NCOs as GOs; most of our men went to the Kalibahadurs as Tom Scott was their Senior Supervising Officer.

The War was brought home to us when John Hudson and Prendergast of the 4/15th received orders to proceed forthwith to Norway as part of a party of ten IA officers being sent to advise on warfare in a mountainous country. As they were not expected to return in the foreseeable future, I became Adjutant at last. Before he left John performed a notable service to the Battalion. It seemed possible that Walter's seniority would cause him to be ordered off on promotion any minute and, as he was present as 2 i/c, Nick would succeed as CO – this, of course, would have been a disaster. John suggested to Walter that, as Ray Selby of the 1st Battalion was senior to Nick, he should be transferred to us ready to take over when he, Walter, left. This was represented to Higher Authority who agreed so Ray arrived and in due course took command; Nick subsequently obtained command of the newly raised 3/6th Gurkhas, who never forgave us.

CHAPTER XIII

Landi Kotal – May–December 1940

Adjutant, Law Course, on notice for an appointment overseas,
Beryl leaves me, and I leave the Battalion

RAY SELBY WAS FIRMLY in the saddle by the beginning of May with myself as Adjutant, and Steve Steveney acting as 2 i/c. Ray Selby was by far the best senior officer and the best CO that I encountered during the whole of my service; under him the Battalion settled down and it was entirely due to his leadership that, in spite of many difficulties, it did so well against the Japanese.

The Indian Army, about this time, introduced wartime acting and temporary ranks. The old time scale was continued for substantive promotion but additionally a battalion was given an establishment of Majors and Captains. If there were not enough substantive holders to fill the quota of each rank, the CO could make it up by acting promotions; as senior subaltern I was one of the first to become an acting Captain. During the period of this chapter, McGill and Buchanan left to join our new 3rd Battalion, John Hudson returned from Norway together with Pendergast, both with well earned MCs, but John went off to the Staff College before the year was out. Our two last Regulars, Dewing and Richardson, arrived but did not stay long, going to the new Regimental Centre and 3rd Battalion respectively. To balance them we received four war time officers and one from the Army in India Reserve of Officers; this latter officer, St Martin, was an Anglo Indian, which raised a few eyebrows, particularly as Indian officers did not serve in Gurkha units. He proved to be a good officer in every respect, went with the Battalion to Malaya and survived the Japanese prison camps. As far as I was concerned, I had started the year as a junior officer and finished it as a senior.

The summer climate in the Khyber was one of the nastiest that I experienced during the whole of my time in India. Landi Kotal at 3,000 ft was not high enough to escape the fierce heat of May, the day temperature being over 100°F. There was no monsoon rain but by the middle to end of June clouds built up which sat over the place like the lid on a saucepan, producing a state of hot airlessness, which was most oppressive. This bore particularly hard on the troops who were not entitled to fans or punkahs. We had cases of sentries fainting during night duty; this alarmed the medical authorities, who installed a thermometer on the Guard Room verandah and found that the night temperature never went below 95°F; there was nothing much, however, which could be done about it. There was no real malaria risk as there was no water for the mosquitoes to breed in, but a new hazard, 'sandfly fever', a particularly unpleasant disease, was rife. The sandflies bred in the mud bricks at the base of the barrack huts; a reasonably effective preventative was the application of old engine oil to the base of them.

I sent Beryl up to Kashmir at the beginning of May, following her up on a month's leave and staying in a houseboat on the Nagin Bagh. During my absence, the Battalion took part in an endurance march, which they came out of with flying colours, in spite of three men collapsing with heat exhaustion and one dying. I was lucky to have another two weeks in the hills as I attended an Adjutant's Law Course at HQ Northern Command at Murree. I suppose that it was my family's legal background which caused me to obtain the only 'excellent' report.

We received orders in August to send approximately one third of the Battalion, with a high proportion of GOs and NCOs, to Dehra Dun for the newly raising 3rd Battalion; this involved a lot of work in sorting out and transferring the men's provident accounts, together with a proportion of the Mess and Welfare Funds. To continue the saga, only a month or so later, we had to find another massive draft for the new 4th Battalion. We were unlucky here, as the 9th was the only Regiment of the Gurkha Brigade to have to raise their 4th Battalion in 1940; all the other Regiments raised their 3rd Battalions in 1940 but their 4th in the following year. The exodus of trained men, GOs and NCOs, was made good by posting in men straight from recruit training.

The next bombshell was a signal from Army HQ: 'T/Capt AA Mains placed on ten days notice to proceed overseas in Field Security Police [sic]'. This foxed everyone as no one had any knowledge of what the FSP was; it had not been mentioned at my Intelligence Course. In fact it had been transferred earlier in the year from the Military Police to the Intelligence Corps and renamed the Field Security Service. I learnt some long time after that my destination would have been Iraq in a Force sent to organize a land route to Egypt. Ray Selby gave me immediate leave for a farewell visit to Beryl, who had moved from Kashmir to Murree. On my return I handed over Adjutant to Chris Graham Hogg and sat down to await orders.

No orders came and after some six weeks, my ten days notice was altered to indefinite notice. Meanwhile Beryl came to Peshawar and we decided to part, at least for the time being. Actually it was the end of our marriage; she went to stay with friends in Lahore, where the RAF officer whom she was later to marry was stationed. Ray Selby had told me earlier that as I was unlikely to go to war with them, he could give me no appointment in the Battalion so I became the odd job man with very little to do.

The Landi Kotal Point to Point races were held in September, when I came down riding a line pony and broke a tendon in my knee necessitating a spell in hospital. The Hospital was a modern building and the CO, Colonel Joshi, had joined the IMS before the Great War, when the service was first opened to Indians. A fine doctor and a gentleman, I could not have been in better hands; I was the first occupant of the Officers' Ward as previously sick officers had been sent to Peshawar, as no female nurses were allowed in Landi Kotal. The CMA had objected to a ward, while staffed, lying idle so in future officers had to be treated there unless special nursing care was essential. Joe produced the 'Cook – officers' in front of me and told him that he was to discuss the menu daily and if there were any complaints about his cooking he would get the sack.

In the meantime Brigadier Hickman had been replaced by Brigadier Goddard; Eric Goddard was a real 'ball of fire', very efficient and energetic, but very highly strung which made him difficult to work with. He could be very frightening but Ray Selby was not

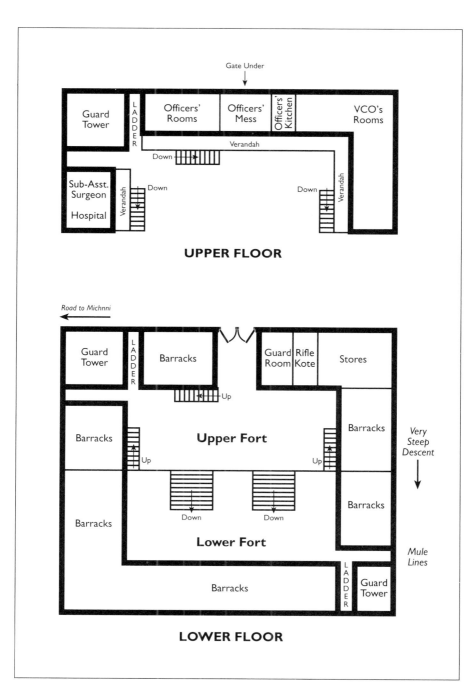

The Khyber, Charbagh Fort.

intimidated by him, neither was Colonel Wilson, the CO of 1/1st Punjab Regiment, a first rate battalion which had replaced the 2/5th Gurkhas. It was different with the 4/15th as Eric, who was really a 'Pffifer', had been sent to command them before O'Morchoe and they had not forgotten it. The BM, Jan Vosper, another Pffifer, also stood in awe of him. When the date of the autumn Column was announced, Jan sent for me and asked if I would volunteer to go out again as Brigade Orderly Officer as I knew the drill and he did not want any slip-ups with the new Brigadier. I agreed, subject to two conditions – first that subject to Ray's approval, I could take a permanent duty platoon from the 2/9th, who were staying in as the Landi Kotal garrison, and second, that I would be responsible only for the running of the Brigade HQ camp and not have to run errands for others. Jan agreed, as did Ray, who thought that a well drilled platoon working under the Brigadier's eye would get good marks for the Battalion. He detailed a really good platoon for the job under a first class Havildar, Katakbahadur Sahi. I had a most enjoyable time – everything went like clockwork and Eric subsequently wrote praising my services and that of the duty platoon. I always got on well with him when later I served with him on the Burma Retreat and in Assam. He finished his service as a Lieutenant General and was the last British GOC in C of Southern Command.

I found the position of odd job man, with few jobs available, very tedious, but I had a bright idea – we were about to take over Charbagh Fort for a two months stint, so I suggested to Ray that I should go as permanent Fort Commander, to which he agreed. All our Company Commanders were now junior to me so command would be no problem. Charbagh was a 'Beau Geste' type Fort. It was built on a hillside which necessitated its construction on two levels and incorporated two guard towers; these were self contained with an entrance by a ladder at first floor level. The Fort's upper area was two storied, with the officers' rooms, Mess and Hospital on the upper floor. As it was overlooked, it had four satellite pickets, Khargali North and South, and Kafir Kot North and South; the north pickets in each case were manned by Khassadars. Kafir Kot can be translated as the 'Foreigner's Fort' and local legend had it that this was the site of one of Alexander the Great's strongholds; in any event, a man-made wall

up with them for many years – Kiran whenever we met insisted on embracing me as his *guru* (teacher) and referring to himself as my *chela* (disciple).

Although I did not know it my time in the Battalion was running out. The Peshawar District Horse Show was held after Christmas and I entered Grave Lady in the Hacks and Polo Pony Classes and my Charger in the Infantry Officers Chargers. I got a 'Highly Commended' in the Polo Pony Class, a good award as I was up against a Cavalry Regiment's ponies, and (I think) a second in the Chargers. At the show I met an officer of District HQ who told me that a posting order for me had come in but he had not himself seen it. Sure enough when I got back to the Battalion, there it was – 'WARNING ORDER. T/Captain A.A. Mains appointed Instructor Class C at Intelligence School being formed at Bombay. Instruct officer to proceed forthwith.' The ambiguity of the order caused some head shaking and was referred back to District who instructed me to move on the 'forthwith'. Meanwhile I had to settle my affairs. The flat was let furnished so there was only the crockery, cutlery and glass to pack up and dispatch to the Regimental Centre for storage, the car I sold, my charger was government responsibility but Joan who was elderly I had put down. Grave Lady I sold for a minimal price to Bill Ridout, who, of course had to pass her on when the Battalion moved – she was in the Regimental Centre in 1942 but afterwards I lost touch with her. Punjab Singh, I paid off with a good chit. Beryl had taken the big Labrador, but I took the other dog, a miniature dachshund, with me. I duly left for Bombay to find that the School was not being formed there but at Karachi. My Record of Service shows that I was struck off the Battalion's books on 18th January 1941, and I was not to return to regimental duty until September 1942 as 2 i/c of the 5th Battalion, which had been raised to replace the 2nd, captured at Singapore.

CHAPTER XIV

Gurkhas and the Gurkha Brigade
of the Indian Army

Note: This Chapter describes the Gurkha and the Gurkha Brigade as I knew them in the 1930s. While there have inevitably been changes, much including the Gurkhas' ethos is still much the same today.

The Gurkha

The term 'Gurkha' stems from the 'Gurkha Army' of Prithvi Narain Shah, the Raja of Gurkha in western Nepal, who, in 1769, overthrew the Malla Kings and made himself master of the Nepal or Khatmandu Valley. He and his successors expanded their jurisdiction westwards along the Himalayan foothills as far as the eastern part of Jammu – that is Kumaon and Garhwal, the Doon Valley, Sirmoor, the Simla Hills and Kangra. They were finally checked by the East India Company who, tiring of border incidents, declared war in 1813. The Treaty of Sagauli which ended the war in 1816, pushed Nepal back to roughly her present boundaries.

The Gurkha Army consisted of the martial clans living in western Nepal – the Thakurs, Khas (Chettris), Magars and Gurungs and it is these clans only who have the absolute right to be called Gurkhas. Later when the Indian Army started to recruit the Kiranti clans, Limbus, Rais and Sunwars from eastern Nepal, the term was applied to all the martial Nepal clans. The Thakurs and Chettris are Khastriyas, or warriors by caste, and wear the sacred thread, while the others are Sudras or peasants.

The Government of Nepal was a curious form of oligarchic dictatorship devised by the first Hereditary Prime Minister and Commander in Chief, Jung Bahadur, who belonged to the Chettri clan of Rana. The King, in 1856, invested him with the title of 'Maharaja' and decreed that the office of Prime Minister be hereditary in his family – on the death of the incumbent to pass to the nearest male relative. This continued until 1950, when the King, who up till then had been merely a religious figurehead, overthrew, with the covert assistance of India, the then Prime Minister and concentrated power in his own person. Meanwhile Jung Bahadur had created a new Chettri clan of Jung Bahadur Rana to cater for his numerous progeny, legitimate and illegitimate.

The Government was almost entirely in the hands of the Chettris – all army officers above captains, all government, municipal and village officials belonged to that clan. The King was a Thakur, which resulted in them receiving preferential treatment, notably being exempted from land revenue.

The Gurkha himself is usually classified as a Mongolian Hindu but their Hinduism is diluted with many Buddhist customs. Most clans have some Aryan admixture, particularly the Chettris, who are sometimes referred to as Gurkha Rajputs, and show this in their facial characteristics of long straight noses and also in their greater stature. The Gurkhas generally are a happy go lucky people, full of fun, but with a slightly bizarre sense of humour, which can be seen in the following true story.

I was supervising the unloading of baggage from a narrow gauge train at Fort Sandeman in the spring of 1945. We found that if we backed a 3-tonner right up to the wagon, we could unload direct from one to the other, a great saving of time and labour. There was a snag – the tailboard grounded as the lorry was being backed up, so it had to be let down at the precise moment that the lorry came up to the door of the wagon. I selected a rifleman to walk back with me holding the tailboard and to drop it when I gave the word. Unfortunately there was an order, that to prevent damage, tailboards should not be dropped but put down gently, so on my order, the rifleman leant forward to put it down slowly. The inevitable happened, the iron stanchion of the lorry got him on one side of his face and the iron wagon on the other. The lorry literally bounced off his head. He went down rolling on the ground and holding his head; could I get any of his buddies to help him? – not so, they were all splitting their sides with laughing at him. Later he got up on his own and I sent him off to the lines for medical treatment. That evening I asked his Company Commander how he was and was told that except for bruises and abrasions he was all right – Gurkha skulls are thick.

The Gurkha fears no one, not even his own officers, and has a very highly developed sense of his superiority over others. He is not as easy to command as some think – it is essential that he has good officers and in my day any British officer who did not measure up to his standards had to be got rid of as soon as possible. His profession may be classified as 'soldier'; as there is no industry in Nepal and the land cannot support the entire population, a large proportion have to enlist – a comparison can be made with the Swiss, who in old times were found in the Armies of France, Naples and the Vatican for the same reason. In my day he despised the Indian plains man and indeed he considered himself superior to any race except the British who were considered as equals. Professor Turner, the expert on the languages of Nepal, who served in the 3rd Gurkhas, recalls sitting overlooking the plains of India when his orderly turned to him and said, 'Look, Sahib, that is the land that I and Thou rule.'

A Gurkha had more fear of the disgrace of being punished for some military offence than of the punishment itself as this would be a loss of face. When I was second in command of the 5/9th, my orderly improperly discharged my revolver; if I sent him to his company commander for punishment, I would lose him as an orderly, so I asked him if he would take a punishment from me. On his agreeing I gave him a sharp tap on the head with the butt of the revolver. He went away rubbing his head but happy – no entry in his sheet roll, none of his friends would know about it, so no apparent disgrace. Of course, it was all highly improper and could have earned me a Court Martial, but it illustrates the trust between British officers and Gurkha soldiers.

Discipline in the Gurkha Brigade, and indeed, in the Indian Army as a whole, was quite different to that in the British Army. The officer was expected to lead in battle and to set an example at all times – he was not expected to interfere with the Gurkha officers in matters of discipline and interior economy. Recruits were assigned to platoons on a village basis so the platoon commander would know the background of his men. I cannot recall any Courts Martial during my time in the 2/9th and very few men brought before their Company Commander for minor misdemeanours. These were dealt with by the

Gurkha officers by unofficial extra guards or fatigues or often by 'one across the ear'ole'. No British officer would check the 'nights in bed' register if it was initiated by the company senior Subedar.

The British Officer was not as close to his men as in the British Army; this was because he did not command a platoon and the GO was specifically placed to act as the link. He was expected to know his GOs and senior NCOs' capabilities and general efficiency, and to keep the CO up to date in this respect. I was handicapped as I was only a company commander during my first year, when my lack of knowledge of Gurkhali was a disadvantage; subsequently I was in HQ as Signals Officer, QM and Adjutant. Our men being Thakurs and Chettris had the 'presence' and good manners of yeoman farmers and lesser squirearchy, unlike the other Gurkhas who might be compared to farm labourers. I always felt when talking to a GO that I was speaking to a social equal.

The Gurkha Brigade
The ten Gurkha Regiments had varied origins – the first three Regiments were raised after the Gurkha War. The Gurkhas were so impressed by the bravery of the British soldier and his fair treatment of prisoners that a number expressed a desire to be taken into the British Forces. The Convention of 1815 stated that any Gurkha soldier could, if he wished, serve in the East India Company's Army. The next Regiment was raised after the Sikh Wars for service in the Punjab Frontier Force and a further one for service in the Mutiny. These five Regiments, from 1861, were numbered separately from the Bengal Infantry as 1 to 5 Gurkha Regiments. The next three Regiments were para-military units raised in the early nineteenth century for service in Assam and the Eastern Frontier, and finally the 9th Bengal and the 10th Madras Infantry were converted into Gurkha units. The Army List showed the class composition of the ten Regiments simply as 'Gurkhas' but the detailed composition was the 9th – Thakurs and Chettris, the 7th and 10th – Kirantis (Limbus, Rais and Sunwars), and the remaining seven Regiments – Magars and Gurungs.

The 'Gurkha Brigade' of ten Regiments each of two Battalions was formed by the combining, between 1901 and 1903, of the existing five Gurkha Regiments with the 9th, 42nd, 43rd and 44th (Gurkha Rifle) Regiments of Bengal Infantry and the 10th (Burma Gurkha Rifle) Regiment of Madras Infantry; these were renumbered as the 9th, 6th, 8th, and 10th Gurkha Rifles respectively, and the arrangement was different to the organization of Indian Infantry of the Line, which consisted, up to 1922, of single battalion Regiments. The term Gurkha Brigade probably came into use at this time. It was entirely unofficial and, indeed, still is in the Indian Army.

The term, therefore, was in general use to denote those ten Gurkha Regiments who were listed separately in the Army List and had a different organization, terms of service and leave rules to other Infantry. Its use may have come about because the Gurkha Brigade was in some respects like the Household Brigade in the British Army i.e. a Corps d'Elite, which was organized differently to other Infantry, and whose Regimental Commanding Officers were found from within the Brigade.

Gurkhas were enlisted also in units outside the Brigade – The Corps of Guides (until 1922), the para-military Assam Rifles and Burma Military Police, the armed forces of the Jammu and Kashmir and Sirmoor Princely States, together with a platoon or so in other States Forces and into the civil Police, notably the Armed sections in Calcutta and Chittagong.

Six Gurkha Battalions were included in the Indian Expeditionary Force to France, and were in the trenches before the end of October 1914, earning the 1914 Star with Clasp '5 Aug–22 Nov' (usually known as the 'Mons Star'). These and the other battalions fought at Gallipoli, and in Egypt, Palestine and Mesopotamia. All but one Regiment raised a 3rd Battalion; seven 3rd Battalions were in action in the 3rd Afghan War of 1919, together with three battalions of a war raised 11th Gurkhas. This expansion and heavy casualties caused reinforcement problems, which necessitated recourse to volunteers from the Assam Rifles and Burma Military Police.

A major reorganization of the Indian Army took place in 1922 when the hundred or more single battalion Regiments were grouped into twenty 'large regiments' usually of five battalions, with a 10th (recruit training) Battalion in a fixed location. The Gurkha Brigade was left unchanged, each battalion having an additional establishment for a training company; this did not accompany the battalion out of the home station but remained as a Depot.

The normal inter-war routine was, or should have been, two years frontier and four years home service, with battalions' service staggered so that both battalions were together for two years in each six. This cycle was interrupted by service in the Moplah rebellion, and in the emergency anti terrorist garrison of Bengal. The situation in the 9th when I joined in 1935 was that both battalions had just returned from Bengal, and the 1st was off almost immediately on its frontier stint.

It was probably unfortunate that some of the Gurkha arrogance towards others had rubbed off on the British officers; like the soldiers they did not think but knew they were the best, and therefore were apt to look down on other regiments. Because of the 1815 Convention, they were not affected by Indianization, and were apt to consider themselves as a form of 'praetorian guard' which could always be relied on, even if the rest of the Indian Army disintegrated as a result of political pressures. There were always more candidates than vacancies so regiments could pick and choose their officers. Many cadets expressed a preference for Gurkhas while still at Sandhurst and others were assured of a vacancy through family connections. I was very lucky, as I had expressed a preference for cavalry for which there was no vacancy, and only got Gurkhas as the 2/9th, very under strength, had turned down two candidates on vetting. In their place I was selected, but I had to keep quiet that Gurkhas had not been my original preference. The Retention Examination was used, rightly or wrongly, to get rid of any young officer who did not match up to the regiment's standards. The examination was conducted by a regimental board who would merely tell the candidate that he would pass only if agreed to put in for a transfer.

The rest of the Indian Army looked upon the Gurkha Brigade with a mixture of dislike and envy; this was by no means unique as in the British Army, then and now, Corps d'Élite can be disliked – examples are the Paras and the Greenjackets, the 'Black Mafia' as they are nicknamed; even the British Brigade of Gurkhas is not universally popular in Service circles.

I will admit that I was, and still am, immensely proud that I should have been selected to serve in a Gurkha Regiment; even today when stating that you served in Gurkhas, one hears 'Oh!' or 'I couldn't quite match that.' A taxi driver once refused to take a fare from me on hearing that I was a retired officer of Gurkhas. On the other hand my service in security intelligence with contacts with other regiments, the civil administration and police, and not least, friendship with Indian officers of these services, led to a considerable change of attitude.

CHAPTER XV

Finale

Exit the British 9th Gurkha Rifles
The Regiment's Services in World War II

Enter the Indian 9th Gorkha Rifles
*The Gurkha Brigade Partitioned – the Regiment's
post Independence Services*

The British 9th Gurkha Rifles

The 2nd Battalion remained in Landi Kotal until 23rd March when they left for Secunderabad to join the 28th Brigade of 6th Indian Division for intensive training, prior to going overseas; there they joined the 1st Battalion who were in 26th Brigade of the same Division. The Division's destination was to be the Middle East, so the training was based on desert conditions involving the use and maintenance of MT.

The Division, including the 1/9th, did in fact finally embark for Iraq, but the 28th Brigade was detached and sent to Malaya as part of the 11th Indian Division. Thanks to Ray Selby, morale was high but the Battalion was being asked to walk before it could crawl – sixty per cent of the riflemen had less than six months service, many GOs and senior NCOs had climbed the promotion ladder twice in the last few months and 175 drivers and motor cyclists had been trained from scratch. Twelve British officers went with the Battalion, five of whom were regulars; Ray Selby, and Maurice Allsebrook returned from the SUL, were Great War veterans, but the third senior, Leslie Young, had only five years service. The Battalion fought a long rearguard action from North Malaya, until finally captured on Singapore Island, but for some reason only one Honour, Malaya 1941–42, was awarded. Five BOs were killed, including my friends Chris Graham-Hogg and Bill Ridout; Leslie Young escaped captivity as he was one of the single

BOs from each battalion who were ordered out before the end; he subsequently raised 'G Gurkha Force' an outshoot of Force 136. According to custom, the Battalion was struck off the Army List until the end of the War, when the remnants were absorbed into the 5/9th as a reconstituted 2/9th. Its last duty before Independence was internal security in the Amballa area of the Punjab under the command of 'Setu' White.

The 1st Battalion was in the same state when it went overseas, but in contrast to the 2nd, it was not sent directly into action, but was employed in a garrison role in Iraq, Syria and Palestine, where it had time to train and sort itself out. When it joined 4th Indian Division just after the Battle of El Alamein, it was a first class unit in every respect. It fought in Libya, Tunisia, Italy and Greece; the action at Hangman's Hill at Cassino will go down as one of the epic battles of the Italian campaign; later at San Marino, Rifleman Sherbahadur won the Victoria Cross. All told the Battalion received ten Battle Honours. John Hudson brought it back to India and it was later employed in the Punjab Boundary Force under the command of Schultze Keily.

The 3rd Battalion after a shakedown tour on the Frontier joined the 14th Indian Division in the Arakan and later was withdrawn to be employed as Divisional Troops in the 3rd Indian Division (the Chindits), where it joined the 4th who had been selected to join the 111th Indian Brigade. In spite of its name, Chindits was neither Indian nor a Division; due to Wingate's dislike of the Indian Army, the Indian content was four Gurkha Battalions only, the remainder being British or West African. During these operations Major Blaker, who had already gained an MC in the Arakan, won a posthumous Victoria Cross.

Both Battalions needed a lengthy period of leave and reorganization, so by the time they were ready to take the field again, the War in the East was as good as won. The 3rd Battalion, however, was sent to help restore order in Java, where they sustained considerable casualties. They then moved to Malaya and finally to Delhi, where the last British CO, David Amoore, handed over to his Indian relief. The 4th Battalion, under Peter Cane, performed garrison duties in Delhi until disbandment in early 1947. Both Battalions were awarded the Battle Honour 'Chindits 1944'; but the Honour 'North Arakan' for the 3rd

Battalion was never claimed. No Honour was awarded for Java but all ranks of the 3rd Battalion were given the General Service Medal 1918–62 with Clasp S.E. Asia 1945–46.

There was a custom in the Indian Army that a unit lost to the enemy should not be replaced during the same campaign, so to replace the three Gurkha Battalions lost in Malaya, the Maharaja of Nepal was prevailed upon to request the Government of India to raise 5th Battalions of the 1st, 2nd, and 9th Gurkhas to avenge their lost comrades. The 5th Battalion was raised in the Regimental Centre in the summer of 1942 by Steve Steveney; it subsequently had a period of useful if not spectacular service in Baluchistan and later in Wana, where on 1st June 1946, the 5th was formally disbanded and with a few survivors of the Japanese prison camps added, was re-raised as the 2nd Battalion.

THUS ENDED ONE HUNDRED AND THIRTY YEARS
SERVICE WITH THE HONOURABLE EAST INDIA COMPANY
AND SUBSEQUENTLY UNDER THE BRITISH CROWN.

The Indian 9th Gorkha Rifles
The granting of Independence to the former French and Dutch Colonies sounded the death knell of the French African and Colonial Armies and of the Dutch Colonial Army, but, although the old Indian Army was partitioned between India and Pakistan and the Gurkhas between India and Britain, the old names and customs have remained.

It is not the remit of this book to go into the reasons how and why some Gurkha Regiments were allotted to Britain and some retained by India. The 9th, comprising the regular 1st and 2nd and the war time 3rd Battalions, was one of the six regiments remaining in the Indian Army; the 4th and 5th Battalions were re-raised in 1951 and 1963 respectively. The only other changes in these early years were the alteration of the Regiment's title to the 9th GORKHA RIFLES, and the formation of a joint Regimental Centre with the 3rd Gurkhas in our Birpur Lines, the 39th Gorkha Training Centre. Most regrettably these Lines were required later for Field Army troops and the Centre was relocated at Varanasi in 1976.

The most daunting task facing the Regiment in 1947 was a

complete changeover of officers, British to Indian. Unlike Indian
Cavalry and Infantry, who had had a proportion of Indians, Gurkhas
had been officered solely by British officers. If there was to be a
smooth changeover it was essential that India provided really good
replacements.

Fortunately there were two sources ready to hand. The first was the
relatively small number of ethnic Gurkhas who were Indian nationals
and who had been granted war time commissions in regiments
outside of the Gurkha Brigade; they were rounded up in the summer
of 1947 and reposted to Gurkha regiments. The second source was
the Hindu and Sikh officers, whose regiments were going to Pakistan
and who were being transferred to Indian regiments. Most of these
officers were excellent material and above the general average.

Indianization was hardly complete when the 3rd Battalion was air
lifted into Poonch to reinforce the besieged Indian garrison. Later the
1st Battalion was engaged in the same sector. The next Battalion to
see action was the 2nd who, in 1958, were engaged in counter
insurgency operations in Nagaland.

The 1st Battalion took part in the China War; they had just
completed a tour in NEFA and were actually on a railway station
platform in Assam, preparing to entrain, when they were turned
round and sent up to the Tibet border at 17,000 ft, still in their
summer uniforms, where they were overrun by superior Chinese
forces. After losing half the battalion, the remnants managed to seek
safety in Bhutan. It is regrettable that this action, the Battle of Thagla
Ridge, did not qualify for a Battle Honour, as India does not award
Honours for defeats, however gallant. This same ruling has deprived
the 2nd Battalion of its possible Malayan Honours in World War II,
while 2/2 GR, whose Honours were gazetted by Britain, were
awarded them.

The 1965 India–Pakistan War saw all Battalions, except the Fourth,
engaged and all except the Fifth in the 1971 War. All told the
Regiment has earned three Honours together with the Theatre
Honours – PUNJAB 1965, PUNJAB 1971, EAST PAKISTAN 1971,
and J & K 1971.

It is extremely gratifying that the Regiment settled down quickly
with its new officers, and to learn of their affection for their Gurkha

soldiers. The Gurkha Brigade has continued to be recognized as a Corps d'Élite and the 9th's prestige is as high as ever. The regimental Esprit de Corps is shown by the fact that recently four Commanding Officers and one Second in Command were sons of earlier Indian COs. Cordial relations have existed between the Regiment and the Regimental Association of former British Officers in the United Kingdom from 1947 until the present day.

The First Railway Journey

OUR SPECIAL WAS drawn up at the platform of Ballard Pier Station and I had my first glimpse of an Indian passenger train. It consisted of three first and second class composites and a brake van; the coaches looked different to those I had been accustomed to in Europe, as they were considerably shorter, and, of course, wider as they were on the 5 ft 6 in gauge. Each coach, an 'FSQ' in railway parlance, had only two first class coupés, each with an upper and lower transverse berth, a first class four berth with upper and lower fore and aft berths, and two second class five berth compartments together with a small compartment with hard wooden seats for servants. Ishaque was standing at the door of one of the coupés, and I found that my stable companion would be Evan Rowland Jones, who had been in the same company at Sandhurst, and was also going to Sialkot. He had been partially educated in India so his advice on rail travel was invaluable. The compartment had a leather covered lower berth and a cane bottomed chair, with the upper berth folded away. There was a small table with a mirror above fixed to the bulkhead, together with a door leading to the bathroom. This had a basin, a WC and a shower, but with cold water only and there was no form of heating. I now knew the reason for the bedding roll which the Army had provided me with as bedding was not supplied. There was, of course, no corridor nor vestibule as each compartment was self contained. At the head of the train was an elderly BB&CI 4-6-0 Locomotive of Class 'HP' built in the Edwardian era. We were informed that the dinner stop would be at Bandra in north Bombay where we would be attached to the main portion of the Mail, which contained the dining car.

At about 7 pm we pulled out onto the main line of the Bombay Port Trust Railway, which we followed to the northern end of the docks where we joined the GIP Harbour Branch, passed over the main line of that railway to reach the BB&CI main line at Bandra. A short walk down the platform to the dining car, for the usual railway dinner – soup, fried fish, roast chicken and caramel custard. An hour later the train stopped for us to regain our compartment. The two servants had been travelling in it, both to look after our belongings and to make up the beds. Evan initiated me into the mysteries of the three window coverings – glass, wire gauze, and wooden venetian – and explained that, however hot it might be, the venetian must be shut and bolted at night, as must the door, as a precaution against thieves. There was no air conditioned stock at that time but all upper class compartments had electric fans and in summer an 80 lb block of ice could be placed in the compartment to help keep it cool. Conversely in certain parts of north India it was the lack of heating which was the problem when, in winter, there were hard frosts at night.

The next morning came tea and toast to our compartment and the news that breakfast would be at the next stop, Ratlam; once again we detrained and our servants took over to roll up the beds and tidy up. I went forward to have a look at the locomotive and found we now had a new Pacific of Class 'XC', for the hilly section through which we were now passing. Another departure from European practice was a driver and two firemen. As was usual in the top links, the driver was an Anglo Indian and the firemen Indians. At the next stop the engine uncoupled and went forward to coal underneath a mechanical coal stage – I believe this was the only example of this in India outside of a loco shed, and was there to avoid changing engines at Ratlam, although crews were changed. The reason was to allow the more powerful 'XC' class engine to go through over the hilly part of the line, otherwise one crew one engine was normal in the Mail links. Towards afternoon engines were changed and we once again got a 'HP' for the flat run to Delhi. At Muttra we left the BB&CI metals and ran the last eighty miles to Delhi by a running power over the GIP main line.

We had lunched on the train and tea had been brought to our compartment, but we arrived at Delhi too early for dinner, which was taken in the station refreshment room; a similar meal to that on the train the evening before. Meanwhile our train was being remarshalled

– it was usual in those days to keep the Mail trains very light partly by the exclusion of third class passengers and partly by severe distance restrictions on intermediate class (a superior type of third class). The Frontier Mail on a normal day would consist of a postal sorting carriage, a brakevan, one FSQ, and one intermediate carriage for Peshawar; the remainder, consisting of the dining car, two FSQs and a composite inter and brakevan, would come off at Delhi and be replaced by an equivalent number of North Western Railway coaches, but no dining car as that would be attached at Lahore on the following morning.

The Delhi stop was of about two hours so there was plenty of time to look around after dinner. There were coaches of four railways to be seen. BB&CI – yellow and brown; GIP – plum; East Indian – green; and North Western – red. We left about 9 pm behind another elderly locomotive a North Western 'E1' class Atlantic which would take us to Lahore; there, the next morning, we acquired a dining car in time for breakfast and two class 'SP' 4-4-0s as motive power. We reached Wazirabad Junction at midday and changed into the branch train of somewhat elderly and decrepit coaches hauled by a goods engine, a class SG 0-6-0, the maid of all work on Indian Railways. We arrived at Sialkot at lunch time and so ended my first journey – a distance of about 1,000 miles which had taken some 42 hours.

Organization of the Army in India – 1935

THE ARMY IN INDIA was organized geographically into Commands, Districts and Brigades.

There was no Divisional organization, but one District in each Command was earmarked as a Divisional Headquarters on mobilization.

Brigades were classified as Field Army, Frontier or Internal Security:

Field Army Brigades were identified by a number and geographical title, e.g. 1st (Abbottabad) Infantry Brigade.

Frontier Brigades were identified by a geographical title only, e.g. Kohat Brigade.

Internal Security Brigades were designated Brigade Areas, e.g. Lahore Brigade Area.

NORTHERN COMMAND (Rawalpindi)

    Rawalpindi District (1st Indian Division)

        1st (Risalpur) Cavalry Brigade

        1st (Abbottabad) Infantry Brigade

        2nd (Rawalpindi) Infantry Brigade

        3rd (Jhelun) Infantry Brigade

    Peshawar District

        Landi Kotal Brigade

        Peshawar Brigade

        Nowshera Brigade

    Kohat District

        Thal Brigade

        Kohat Brigade

    Waziristan District

        Razmak Brigade

        Wana Brigade

Lahore District
  2nd Sialkot Cavalry Brigade[1]
  Lahore Brigade Area
  Jullundur Brigade Area
  Ferozepore Brigade Area
  Amballa Brigade Area

WESTERN COMMAND[2] (Quetta)
  Baluchistan District (2nd Indian Division) (Quetta)
    4th (Quetta) Infantry Brigade
    5th (Quetta) Infantry Brigade
  Sind (Independent) Brigade Area

EASTERN COMMAND (Bareilly)
  Meerut District (3rd Indian Division) (Dehra Dun)
    3rd (Meerut) Cavalry Brigade
    7th (Dehra Dun) Infantry Brigade
    8th (Bareilly) Infantry Brigade
    9th (Jhansi) Infantry Brigade
  Lucknow District
    6th (Lucknow) Infantry Brigade (Army HQ reserve)
    Allahabad Brigade Area
  Presidency and Assam District (Calcutta)
    Eastern Bengal Brigade Area
  Delhi (Independent) Brigade Area

SOUTHERN COMMAND (Secunderabad)
  Deccan District (4th Indian Division) (Secunderabad)
    4th (Secunderabad) Cavalry Brigade
    10th (Jubbulpore) Infantry Brigade
    11th (Ahmednagar) Infantry Brigade
    12th (Secunderabad) Infantry Brigade
  Bombay District
    Mhow Brigade Area
  Madras District.
  Poona (Independent) Brigade Area

BURMA (INDEPENDENT) DISTRICT[3]

Notes:

1. The 2nd (Sialkot) Cavalry Brigade was abolished in 1935, and became the Sialkot Brigade Area.
2. Western Command was abolished in 1938 and reorganized as:
    Western (Independent) District
        Quetta Brigade
        Zhob Brigade
        Khojak Brigade
        Sind Brigade Area
3. On the separation of Burma from India in 1935, Burma District ceased to be part of the Army in India and became the nucleus of Headquarters BURMA ARMY.

Dehra Dun

D EHRA DUN IS SITUATED in the centre of the Doon Valley, in the foothills of the Himalayas, about 140 miles north of Delhi. The valley lies at an altitude of just over 2,000 ft and is positioned between the Siwalik Range of foothills rising to about 3,000 ft and the first range of the Himalayas proper at over 6,000 ft.

The valley itself is about sixty miles long and ten to fifteen wide and is drained by rivers flowing to the Jumna (Yamuna) in the west and the Ganges (Ganga) in the east. These two rivers flow across the ends of the valley at the point where they break through the Siwalik Range into the plains of north India. The actual watershed is at Dehra itself. The various rivers in the valley rise in the foothills of the Himalayan range and flow south in very deep and narrow gorges until they reach the floor of the valley, when they turn to east or west to join either the Ganges or the Jumna. Between these rivers lie narrow plateaux rising gently up to the Himalayas proper. Much of the valley is forested and between the Wars abounded in big game, tigers, elephants and panthers as well as sambhur and cheetal.

In spite of its altitude, Dehra was not a hill station, but its climate had some advantages over stations in the north Indian plains. In the first place, although fans were necessary in the hot weather, the maximum temperature was not so high, 105°F as against 115°F in the plains. The other advantage was that the hot weather started nearly a month later and ended earlier.

A major feature of Dehra Dun were two sizeable minorities. In Dehra town, there was a considerable number of domiciled Europeans and Anglo Indians; they were mostly retired civil, police and railway officers or planters. The other minority were Gurkhas, originally pensioners from the 2nd Gurkhas, who had been given grants of land on retirement.

Until the end of the Gurkha War in 1816, the valley was part of the

Kingdom of Nepal. One of the three original Battalions of Gurkhas raised from the defeated Nepal Army, the Sirmoor Regiment, later the 2nd Gurkhas, was located at Dehra Dun in barracks on what later became the Maidan, in close proximity to Dehra City. The hill station of Mussoorie was established in 1823, but the cart road from the plains, opened in the following year, terminated about four miles north of Dehra at the village of Rajpur, where the hill bridleway commenced. A number of hotels and posting houses grew up there to cater for the transhipment of travellers from wheeled vehicles to ponies and dhoolies. The Survey of India established its Headquarters in Dehra Dun shortly afterwards, followed by the Governor General's Bodyguard, who, in 1831, built lines on the Rajpur Road, for occupation in the summer only. The growth of Dehra made the original 2nd Gurkhas' lines very cramped so in 1869, the Cantonment was moved westward over the Bindal River to the plateau between it and the Tons.

The railway arrived from Hardwar about 1900, and subsequently the Imperial Cadet Corps was located in an area just south of the 2nd Gurkhas. The Dehra Dun Brigade was formed by the arrival of the 9th Gurkhas and two Mountain Batteries in 1905; there was no room for them in the Cantonment so they were situated further west on the plateau between the Tons and Noon rivers. The 9th were encamped on the eastern side near the evacuated village of Birpur, where they built their own Lines, Bungalows and Mess. The Mountain Gunners were accommodated on the western side at the village of Ghangora. The location of these units necessitated the building of a a road from the Cantonment, the Tons River gorge being crossed by a very high girder bridge. Other, post Great War, developments were the arrival of Headquarters Meerut District (3rd Indian Division), the Indian Military Academy, the Forest Research Institute and the Doon School.

Dehra Dun can be divided into:

The City and Civil Lines
This was one of three plateaux, lying to the east of the Bindal River, which finally flowed into the Ganges. The City itself was very small, no bigger than the Saddar Bazaar of a large Cantonment. The railway station was on the main road to the plains immediately south of it.

North of the City was the junction of the Chakrata and Mussoorie Roads. The Mussoorie road continued north through the Civil Lines to the Control Gate at Rajpur, the commencement of the motor hill road to Mussoorie.

The part of the Civil Lines immediately north of the crossroads comprised the Maidan, the main Post and Telegraph Office, the Dehra Dun Club, and the main shopping centre. The main block of shops (Astley Hall) was more akin to a shopping street in Europe than to an Indian Bazaar. Further up the road, both astride it and to the east, was the main residential area, well to do bungalows with gardens watered by one of the small canals running down from the foothills. There was no garrison Church as such − both the Churches were in the Civil Lines, the Anglican on the Rajpur Road and the Catholic at the south east corner of the Maidan.

To the south east of the Maidan was the suburb of Dalanwala, an area of smaller bungalows inhabited mainly by retired Anglo Indians with their own Club. A few military and government agencies were located in the Civil Lines − notably the Headquarters and Armoury of the Dehra Dun Contingent of the Auxiliary Force (India), the Headquarters of the Meerut (Military) District and the Survey of India; also located here were the summer quarters of the Viceroy's Body Guard and the Stallion Stables of the Army Remount Department.

The Chakrata Road ran due west through a very narrow bazaar street, always crowded with people and known to many officers as 'Suicide Bazaar'. After crossing the Bindal river, it divided, the Cantonment Road running up the plateau between the Bindal and Tons Rivers and the Chakrata Road continuing west to the Forest Research Institute and Indian Military Academy. This was the watershed as the Bindal flowed east to the Ganges and the Tons west to the Jumna.

The Cantonment
The cantonment was the preserve of the 2nd Gurkhas − the Mess and the lines of the 1st Battalion in the southern portion and the 2nd Battalion's further up the plateau to the north of the Brigade parade ground, which was used as a relief polo ground. The 2nd Gurkhas

maintained their own polo ground as well as a nine hole golf course, with greens instead of the usual baked earth 'browns'. Brigade Headquarters, the Combined Indian Military Hospital, the AT Lines and the Supply Depot were also situated in the cantonment. The old Imperial Cadet Corps Lines were now occupied by the Prince of Wales Royal Indian Military College – organized as a militarized public school, it was designed to prepare Indian boys for entry into Woolwich or Sandhurst. The Doon School, the 'Eton of India', was opened in the old Forest College in 1936. The Government of the United Provinces maintained a Circuit House in cantonments. This was a magnificent thatched bungalow with a large and beautiful garden; known as Doon Court, it was a favourite resort of the Viceroy to escape from the hurley-burley of the hill moves of the Government of India.

Birpur and Ghangora
This area lies on a plateau immediately north of the junction of the Tons and Noon Rivers. The enlargement of the garrison of Dehra Dun from two Gurkha Battalions to a Brigade meant that, while the Brigade Headquarters and ancillary units could be accommodated in the Cantonment, there was no room for the two Battalions of the 9th Gurkhas or the two Mountain Batteries. A decision thus was taken to locate them in the area to the west, although this would entail the construction of a new road and a major bridge over the Tons River.

Birpur
The road to Birpur and Ghangora runs west out of the Cantonment through the village of Garhi, and then comes down the side of the Tons Gorge to a high girder bridge, known unofficially as the 'Bridge of Sighs'. Across the bridge the Ghangora road continues west along flat ground, past the Veterinary Hospital, but the Birpur Road turns north and begins to climb up the plateau through the regimental family quarters. The actual battalion lines were situated on either side of the road with the battalion offices at the top. Passing the polo ground, officially built as a parade ground, and the officers' bungalows, the road ends at the Mess. This is situated on a promontory overlooking the Tons valley, and with a view of

Mussoorie some 4,000 feet above. Many have said that this is the finest situation of any Mess in India.

Ghangora
Ghangora is separated from Birpur by a shallow valley and overlooks the Noon River. The road passes by the lines of the Mountain Batteries to terminate at the Royal Artillery Mess and a few officers' bungalows. There was an open space where the British Battalion from Chakrata used to encamp in the winter months. An unmade road once joined Birpur and Ghangora, but when a bridge in the valley was washed away the Military Engineering Service thought the road unnecessary and did not repair it, leaving it unfit for wheeled traffic.

The Forest Research Institute and the Indian Military Academy
These two establishments were situated adjacent to each other, about five miles west of the City.

The Forest Research Institute
The Institute proper is a handsome red brick building, with the laboratories and officers' bungalows adjacent, all in its own park, and containing an eighteen hole golf course. A feature of the park was the 'Jacaranda Avenue', which when the trees were in flower was a sight to remember.

The Indian Military Academy
The IMA is adjacent to the south. Originally the Railway Staff College, the main feature of the buildings is the Chetwode Hall, named after the Commander in Chief in 1932, when the Academy opened.

Frontier Columns

Introduction

A 'FRONTIER COLUMN', as it was known in the period 1922 to 1947, was the movement of a body of troops through Tribal Territory away from a motor road. This might be part of a punitive mission or merely to show the flag.

The column, usually of a Brigade (of two or three battalion strength) with supporting arms was of very considerable length as everything – baggage, rations, forage, ammunition etc – had to be carried on mules, except in Baluchistan, where the camels of the two Silladar Camel Transport Companies might be employed. I did four columns, three in 1939–40 from Landi Kotal and one in 1944 from Fort Sandeman. On my first column I was Quartermaster of the 2/9th Gurkhas, the second and third found me attached to Brigade HQ as Brigade Orderly Officer (assistant to the Staff Captain and responsible for the administration of Brigade HQ), and as second in command of the 5/9th Gurkhas on the last. The only difference in the make up of the columns was that the last had regimental 3" mortars and there had been a limited issue of 'walkie-talkies', otherwise the supporting arms were regimental MMGs and mountain artillery, and the signalling equipment, flag, lamp and helio.

In spite of the territory being well mapped, a column's progress was very slow and a day's march was not much above five or six miles or less if opposition was encountered. This was conditioned by the length of the column, the necessity of piqueting all overlooking heights and of arriving at the camp site in time to build a perimeter wall before dark.

The March – Piqueting

Piqueting had become a science, handed down from unit to unit and in the case of Gurkha regiments, with their frontier tour every fifth year, assiduously practised during their 'home' service. In every case the 'Piqueting Officer' was the CO of the battalion providing the advance guard; Brigade HQ would be in the centre with the reserve. There were two schools of thought over the duration of the Piqueting Officer's tour of duty – one was that the original Piqueting Officer and advance guard remained for the whole march, using men of other battalions as piquets when his own were used up, the other that when the Piqueting Officer's battalion was used up, the advance guard and Piqueting Officer was found by the next battalion in rotation.

The Piqueting Officer's 'O' Group would consist of himself, his Adjutant and Signal Officer, with representatives of the supporting arms, together with the platoon and section commanders of the first company to be used. On arrival at the area to be piqueted, the column would halt and the Piqueting Officer, having decided which peaks were to be piqueted, would order 'No 1 LEFT one section' (odd number piquets to the left, even to the right), indicating the position to the piquet commander with his pointer staff; the gunner, machine gunner and mortar commander then had the piquet position pointed out to them. Meanwhile the adjutant was making out the piqueting slips – these came in booklets with two detachable portions and a counterfoil and recorded the piquet number, strength and unit finding it. One portion was given to the piquet commander and the second was sent back to the rearguard commander. After the route had been piqueted for some distance the column would move on, and the procedure would be repeated at the next halt.

It was usual for each piquet to include a signaller with flag, and the commander himself would have an identifying flag and white air identification strips; the former would be displayed in view of the column, the latter in the form of a cross to identify the picket from the air and in event of an attack changed to a 'T', the long piece pointing towards the enemy.

The rearguard commander's 'O' group was similar to the piquet commander's, with the addition of a large red flag carried by an orderly; so no one got left behind, everyone other than the rear guard troops had to be in front of this flag. The rear guard commander was responsible for calling down the piquets, when their task was finished. This was done by flag, morse or semaphore, or sometimes by using the red flag itself, giving the 'wash out signal' followed by indicating the piquet number by waves of the flag. The supporting arms would be ready to fire onto the piquet's position as soon as all the men were off it, the piquet commander coming off last waving his flag. On arrival back at the column, he would report his piquet 'all accounted for' and would give up his piqueting slip which would be compared with the rearguard commander's slip to ensure that no piquet was overlooked. The advance guard and rear guards performed the functions usual in any operation – the advance guard, in extended order, sweeping the valley ahead of the column and the rearguard ready to halt and turn about to repel any attack from the rear.

The Camp

Note: The layout of a camp could vary according to the ideas of the Brigade/Column Commander; I have described the camps and battalions which I was in (2/9 GR Landi Kotal and 5/9 GR Fort Sandeman).

As soon as the camp site was reached, the column, still protected by the last piquets put up during the march, would halt and the Staff Captain with his camp party would go forward and site the camp, using flags and pegs. There were only two rules: one was to place the infantry around the perimeter and the second to make each of the gates a responsibility of one unit. When this was done, he would call in the unit QMs with their camp parties, and indicate their respective areas. They in their turn would lay out their unit areas. In my regiment, the QM had a mule laden with flags, pegs and coloured rope; the company areas were ringed with ropes of the company colours. Finally, guides were sent to bring in the battalions.

On arrival arms were grounded and equipment taken off with sentries posted; to rest their feet the men removed their boots and put on the gym shoes which they were carrying in their packs. Then everyone who could be spared got down to finding boulders to make a breast high wall. Officers' orderlies relieved their officers of their equipment, except for their revolvers. Most officers had their issue leather holsters attached to a web bandolier with spaces for the bullets; this could be worn over the shoulder in lieu of their equipment.

The transport animals would now come in and dump their loads, greatcoats, blankets, rations, ammunition and water, going out again to feed and water and staying out until dusk; with them came the followers, cooks, water carriers and sweepers, also the mess servants with the mess mule. Some time later the column commander would call a conference to review the day's events and to give orders for the night routine and for striking camp the next morning. It is not possible to recount all the various activities going on: building the wall, laying out night lines for the supporting arms, relieving the day piquets by the night ones, and so on – a hive of activity until 'stand to' at dusk, when everyone, fully equipped and armed, would take up his night emergency position. During the night officers and men slept with their arms by them, the men's rifles being chained to them. The reserve, known as the 'inlying piquet', slept fully equipped and armed, and, of course, sentries were on watch at intervals round the wall. The troops bivouaced with their greatcoats, blankets and groundsheets. In most Indian regiments, the officers had lightweight shelter tents. If there was a possibility of hostile snipers the tents were dug down.

Specialized Equipment
There was a great deal of specialized equipment provided at unit or officer's expense. When I joined the 2/9th from my attachment to a British Regiment, I had to provide myself with a set of officer's pattern Mills Web Equipment, a lightweight Hounsfield bed, a shelter tent, a sleeping bag and a pointer staff. The Mess had a lightweight tent and special lightweight yakdans; these had straps on the top, one for a primus stove, the other for a kettle so that the Mess butler, who went with it, could brew up before the arrival of the rest of the transport. Regimental equipment was the flags, pegs and coloured rope for marking out the camp area.

Frontier Glossary
Note: A mule load was 1 maund (80 pounds) each side.

Yakdan	a leather container
Pakhal	a felt covered water container
	both designed to fit on one side of a pack saddle.
Chaghal	a canvas water container (about 2 pints) either carried or hung on a pack saddle; the canvas being porous allowed evaporation which kept the water cool.

Khajawah   a stretcher designed to fit on one side of a pack saddle.
Pointer staff   two straight pieces of wood or metal joined in parallel
                with a handle on one and rifle sights on both, used to
                indicate targets.

Indian Army Ranks – 1935

Note: These ranks refer to dismounted Corps only.

Viceroy's Commissioned Officers

These officers wore a Sword and were saluted by Indian other ranks, but were junior to King's Commissioned Officers.

Subedar Major	wearing a crown
Subedar	wearing two stars
Jemadar	wearing one star

Warrant and Non Commissioned Officers

Indian Rank	*British equivalent*
Battalion Havildar Major★ (BHM)	RSM
Battalion Quartermaster Havildar★ (BQMH)	RQMS
Company Havildar Major★ (CHM)	CSM
Company Quartermaster Havildar★ (CQMH)	CQMS
Havildar	Sergeant
Naik	Corporal
Lance Naik	Lance Corporal

★These were appointments in the Indian Army, not ranks – the holder's substantive rank was Havildar. There were no Warrant ranks.

Glossary

Terms and Abbreviations

ADC	Aide de Camp
A or AG	Adjutant General's Branch
APA	Assistant Political Agent
AT	Animal Transport
BB&CI	Bombay, Baroda and Central India (Railway)
BM	Brigade Major
BOR	British Other Rank
BT	For the use of British troops
Cantonment	Indian military town
Chowkidar	Watchman
CIGS	Chief (of the) Imperial General Staff
CMA	Controller of Military Accounts
CO	Commanding Officer
CQMS	Company Quartermaster Sergeant
CSM	Company Sergeant Major
Conductor	Warrant Officer 1st grade (IA only)
Daffadar	Cavalry Sergeant
Dak Bungalow	Travellers' bungalow providing beds and food
DCM	Distinguished Conduct Medal
Doaba	Flat area on either side of large river
ERE	Extra regimentally employed
FSQ (Railway)	Coach with I, II and servants' accommodation
Furlough	Leave on half pay
GIP	Great Indian Peninsula (Railway)
GO	Gurkha Officer (see VCO)

GOR	Gurkha Other Rank
GR	Gurkha Rifles
GSO II	General Staff Officer 2nd Grade
Hill station	Cantonment in the mountains for hot weather occupation
H(I)PA	Hurlingham (Indian) Polo Association
IA	Indian Army
IACC	Indian Army Corps of Clerks
ICS	Indian Civil Service
IDC	Imperial Defence College
IMS	Indian Medical Service
Indian Army ranks	see Appendix E
IT	For the use of Indian troops
HM's	His Majesty's
Jemadar Adjutant	Assistant Adjutant
JUO	Junior Under Officer
KCIO	Kings Commissioned Indian Officer
Khassadar	Tribal Police
L(M)MG	Light (Medium) Machine Gun
Maidan	Flat, usually grassy, area in a town
Mali	Gardener
MES	Military Engineering Service
MO	Medical Officer
NCO	Non Commissioned Officer
NWFP	North West Frontier Province
OC	Officer Commanding
'O' Group	Orders Group
Overalls	Tight trousers strapped under the instep
Panchayet	Tribunal of five members (*panchh* = 5)
Patrols	Undress uniform jacket – blue except rifle green for Rifle regiment
Pffifer (PFF)	Punjab Frontier Force
PM	Punjabi Mussulman
PT	Physical Training
QM	Quarter Master
Quarter Master Jemadar	Assistant Quarter Master
RAEC	Royal Army Educational Corps

RAF	Royal Air Force
Rest House	Travellers' bungalow – beds only
RGR	Royal Gurkha Rifles
RMC	Royal Military College
RSM	Regimental Sergeant Major
Roll on my boat (slang)	Hurry up my repatriation/discharge
Sheet roll	Soldier's record of service
Silladar	Unit in which drivers provided their own animals
SB (belt)	Sam Browne
Shikara	Taxi boat on Srinagar lakes
Shikari	Professional hunter
SWBs	South Wales Borderers
Sowar	Cavalry Trooper
SUO	Senior Under Officer
UP	United Provinces
VCO (see Appendix E)	Viceroy's Commissioned Officer
VD	Venereal Disease